Finding Weakness in Jihadist Propaganda

A Monograph
by
MAJOR Timothy R. King
U.S. Army

MENS EST CLAVIS VICTORIAE

School of Advanced Military Studies
United States Army Command and General Staff College
Fort Leavenworth, Kansas

AY 06-07

SCHOOL OF ADVANCED MILITARY STUDIES

MONOGRAPH APPROVAL

Major Timothy King

Title of Monograph: *Finding Weakness in Jihadist Propaganda*

Approved by:

_____   Monograph Director
Michael Mosser, Ph.D.

_____   Director,
Kevin C.M. Benson, COL, AR   School of Advanced
                                              Military Studies

_____   Director,
Robert F. Baumann, Ph.D.   Graduate Degree
                                              Programs

Abstract

Finding Weakness in Jihadist Propaganda by Major Timothy R. King, U.S. Army, 58 pages.

The Global War on Terror is an ideological war being fought in the environment indicative of fourth generation warfare. Propaganda bypasses traditional defenses and strikes right at the center of gravity – popular support. In a modern war of ideologies, communication is decisive; propaganda is cleverly designed, influential communication that compels associated populations to support the cause or leave the battlefield. The Jihadists seek social revolution and rely on propaganda to communicate the cause. Propaganda is especially effective because of the nature of globalized communications – a picture, a video, or a statement quickly consumes the attention of the world media and is spread instantaneously.

Communist China successfully completed a social revolution during the 20th Century. Their revolution has striking similarities to the current Jihadist social revolution. China had a significant capability the Jihadists do not; the Chinese government could control nearly all aspects of information within their country.

Despite the advantages of globalized communications, the Jihadists do not "own" the battlefield. They are effectively using the battleground (television, internet, satellite TV) but pale in comparison to America's potential. Today, America does little to compete with the Jihadists in the realm of information operations. America can win the war of ideology on the information battlefield should it ever decide to compete.

TABLE OF CONTENTS

INTRODUCTION 1

WHAT IS PROPAGANDA? 4

THE CHINESE EXAMPLE 15

THE JIHADIST'S EXAMPLE 27

WEAKNESSES TO EXPLOIT 42

CONCLUSION 51

APPENDIX 1 World War I 53

APPENDIX 2 World War II.. 54

APPENDIX 3 Communist China 55

APPENDIX 4 Jihadist Propaganda 56

BIBLIOGRAPHY 57

INTRODUCTION

The Global War on Terror is a conflict that is much more complex than a coordinated effort to combat crime. The violent attacks on 9/11 preceded by the attacks on the USS Cole, Khobar Towers, U.S. Embassies and other acts of terrorism were not simple hate crimes against America, the world leaders of democracy; they were instead, acts of war committed in Social Revolution against the "American Empire". The age of globalization has ushered in a new world order that is for some undesirable. The advancements in technology has drastically changed the nature of global trade, global communications, and has had a general effect of diffusing civilizations and challenging traditions across cultural lines. The traditionalist enemy of this advancement possesses a contrasting ideology that calls for preservation of the Islamic religion and culture through forceful isolationism from the West – specifically America. Theirs is an ideology that calls for a revitalization of the Islamic Empire through piety, strict religious observance and the defeat of the United States. This ideology is hereafter referred to as the "Global Jihad" and is a product of a social revolution led by terrorist networks much in the same way that historical revolutions fought for power and sovereignty against ruling powers of nation states. Globalization has had an effect of removing borders for trade, communications, and networking; likewise, it has removed the borders for unrestricted warfare for those who understand this reality in the new world order.

The Global Jihad's ideology is weak in logic, and shows no evidence that it is capable of delivering its desired outcomes. The Islamic Civilization[1] is, as compared with the West, underdeveloped. The Global Jihadists have assigned blame for this underdevelopment squarely on the shoulders of the United States. However, their backwardness is not caused by the United States, it is caused by their inability to keep pace with the West and modernize – Islamic philosophers of the 18th to 20th Centuries came to this same conclusion years ago. The United

---

[1] The term "Islamic Civilization" is used in the manner described by Samuel P. Huntington in his book <u>The Clash of Civilizations and Remaking of World Order</u>, (New York: Simon and Schuster, 1996)

States is a scapegoat. The Jihadist's revolutionary philosophy actually calls for the Islamic society to move further backwards by shunning science, Western technology, and modern government for socioreligious reasons. Why then, is it so immensely popular in the Islamic world? Its popularity is based on the general hatred for the United States. Hatred, a very powerful emotion, is derived from many sources such as support for Israel, capitalism, imperialism, perceived arrogance and secularism – all of these "evils" have created a common bond with the "have-nots" of the Middle East. The Global Jihad relies on propaganda to fuel the hatred that unifies Muslims and maintains the movement. Nevertheless, hatred, revenge, and destruction of America are not enough to return the Islamic caliphate. The caliphate's return in the 21st Century is a utopian dream. Jihadist propaganda is emotional and misleading – and, like the ideology it communicates – is full of empty promises.

Jihadist propaganda works and is vital to maintaining the movement. Propaganda spreads hatred, calls for revenge, raises money and recruits disenchanted Muslims to the cause across the globe. It also strikes right at the heart of America; Jihadist propaganda bypasses America's military defenses, hits American public opinion, and influences domestic politics. This propaganda battle is fought in ideological war amidst the environment of "Fourth Generation Warfare"[2]. Ironically, it is this age of globalized communications, i.e. internet, e-mail, international media and satellite television that enable the Jihadists to communicate their revolution's ideas instantaneously. Despite the inherent advantages and convenience of global communications it is also has a huge disadvantage. The disadvantage is the open and free environment of the airwaves. This is an environment where anyone can compete. Jihadists can produce a vast array of videos, images and messages that communicate their ideology to nearly anyone on a global scale; we can do the same, we can communicate too. Historically, this has not always been the case. Before the age of global communications, societies controlled by

---

[2] The concept of Fourth Generation War is explained by William S. Lind and Colonel Keith Nightengale, *The Changing Face of War: Into the Fourth Generation*, Marine Corps Gazette, 1989.

totalitarian regimes were completely cut off from the West and the ideas of democracy and freedom. Social revolution could progress in those states without interference.

The Chinese Revolution of the 20th Century, like the current Global Jihadist movement, was an attempt at social revolution. China's revolution was successful, and because is was, is worth looking at in comparison to today's Jihadist movement. What are the shared characteristics of the Chinese and Jihadist social revolutions? It turns out that there are similarities. Both identify Western imperialism as a cause for their backwardness; both rely on popular support; both rely on terrorism, insurgency and guerilla warfare; and both rely on propaganda. Mao Tse-Tung led a successful revolution in China partly because the communist ideology was a plausible economic solution to the plight of the Chinese people and partly because his propaganda was compelling. Mao, like the Jihadists, left no stone unturned when developing and communicating their ideologies with propaganda. Mao Tse-Tung considered the support of the population essential to China's revolutionary war. In fact, he explained how the Red Army's existence was to further the political ideology of the Revolution; without politics, the actions of the Red Army would become meaningless[3]. In other words, the Red Army exists to spread the ideas of the revolution. However, Mao had one distinct advantage the Jihadists do not – Mao's Red Army (and later the communist government) could completely isolate China's population from the West. The Jihadists cannot accomplish the same. Unfortunately, the West – specifically America – is not taking advantage of this weakness. By comparing these two social revolutions, this monograph will show strengths of Mao's ideology and propaganda as compared with the weaknesses of the Global Jihadist's ideology and propaganda. The advantages of Mao's propaganda in a totalitarian environment are striking when compared with the Jihadist's propaganda in the free and open communications network of today. The monograph is divided into four major divisions: *What is Propaganda* – a definition of propaganda that goes beyond notional understanding, *The Chinese*

---

[3] Mao Tse-Tung, <u>The Selected Works of Mao Tse-Tung, Volume One 1926-1936</u>, (New York: International Publishers, 1954) 106.

Example – a case study of an effective propaganda campaign, *The Jihadist's Example* – current propaganda themes and messages, and *Weaknesses to Exploit* – exposition of the many weaknesses in Jihadist propaganda. The exposed weaknesses in the Jihadist ideology and propaganda must be exploited if we are to succeed in the Global War on Terror.

WHAT IS PROPAGANDA?

A notional understanding

Lies, distortions, fabrications, exaggerations, disinformation, spin, and censorship are words that typically describe propaganda. If propaganda is synonymous with these terms then it is unethical and wrong. These terms are however, examples of a mere notional understanding of propaganda. According to our own Joint Doctrine, propaganda is "*propaganda. Any form of communication in support of national objectives designed to influence the opinions, emotions, attitudes, or behavior of any group in order to benefit the sponsor, either directly or indirectly*"[4]. The civilian equivalent is similar; according to *Dictionary.com*, the definition of propaganda is "*The systematic propagation of a doctrine or cause or of information reflecting the views and interests of those advocating such a doctrine or cause*"[5]. By these accounts, propaganda is neutral. Do we misunderstand propaganda *because of propaganda*? Why does it have such a bad reputation? Is there anything unethical about the propagation of a cause by using information that reflects the views of the advocate? By JP 3-53 and *Dictionary.com's* definitions, it is fair to say that we all are exposed to countless propaganda messages every day. Television programming and advertisements, radio commercials, political campaigning, print ads, "pop-ups" on our computers and junk mail are just a few forms of propaganda we encounter daily – and, it is completely acceptable. Does persuasive information become propaganda simply because it comes

---

[4] Joint Pub 3-53, <u>Doctrine for Joint Psychological Operations</u> 10 July 1996
[5] propaganda. Dictionary.com. *The American Heritage® Dictionary of the English Language, Fourth Edition*, Houghton Mifflin Company, 2004. <u>http://dictionary reference.com/browse/propaganda</u> (accessed: December 01, 2006).

from the government? What about when the nation is at war – do the ends justify the means? What if the message is morally right and factually true – is it still propaganda? The issue with propaganda is that propagandists have shown little regard for truth in the construction of their persuasive messages *and* those we label as propagandists have an opposing ideology to ours. In war, one's patriotic message is another's wartime propaganda; it is perception and perception is reality.

An illustration

In a practical sense, propaganda is a message derived from the combined functions of the Information, Social and Political systems (PMESII model[6]). Propaganda begins with an idea that "needs propagation" – in other words, an ideology for a movement being led for a social or political purpose. These ideologies are usually derived from the Social or Political systems and are communicated through the Information system. The information system

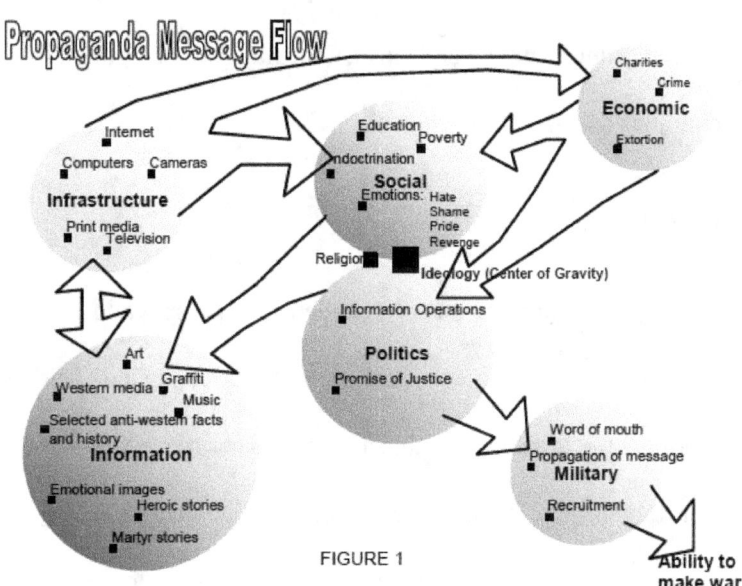

FIGURE 1

communicates individual messages that describe and sell the ideology – those messages are propaganda. By using the PMESII model, we can follow the path of the ideological messages and see how they affect the conflict. In figure 1, propaganda is illustrated as a combat multiplier for the notional cause. Powerful emotions brought on by social conditions look to politics for justice

---

[6] *Commander's Handbook for an Effects-Based Approach to Joint Operations*, Joint Warfighting Center, Suffolk Virginia 2006, ii – 4.

and relief. Political powers use information to propagate the cause using a variety of themes. The information becomes propaganda – biased, inspirational information – that is physically conveyed by the existing infrastructure such as print, television, computer and word of mouth. The internet allows easy propagation of the message to a global audience. A portion of the global community is influenced enough to provide economic and political support to the cause. Some are inspired to join the movement. Money, recruits and ideology allow the political leaders to continue military operations globally. Domestically, in regions of conflict, propaganda messages simplify the combatant societies' notional understanding of the conflict, confirm traditional beliefs, reinforce prejudices and sustain hatred for America and its coalition partners. Collectively the messages persuade the populous to support the movement. Propaganda, as a means of persuading, does not utilize all known facts and is therefore, inherently biased. Propagandists typically sacrifice ethical behavior citing that the "ends justify the means". Categories of propaganda are various as are the techniques used in conveyance.

Ideology

Propaganda starts with an ideology. As said above, propaganda is the use of information to propagate a cause. The "cause" in wartime propaganda is ideology. Propaganda is based on an ideology – the ideology is subject to ethical scrutiny. The word "ideology" sounds as if it has a scientific notion to it – as if it is the study of an idea. In reality however, ideology is simply the logic of the idea as seen through history – that is, history as the ideologist sees it. In the most basic sense, ideology consists of a problem and a solution. Empirical knowledge of totalitarian regimes has shown that they are the predominate users of ideology as a social tool seeking conformity of their societies. Totalitarian ideologies avoid dialog (thesis, antithesis, synthesis) because the totalitarians resist the notion of sharing power; their idea (understanding of the problem and proposed solution) is superior and sufficient. Totalitarian ideologies provide total explanation of the past, total explanation of the present and reliable prediction of the future[7].

Through logic, their ideology offers answers to the problems society is likely to face in the future.

Since there is a lack of dialectic exchange, totalitarian ideology falsely provides complete

answers. Ideology relies on pseudo-logic – logical arguments but only insofar as it supports itself

– it is not true dialog. Contradictions in ideas (antithesis) quickly become conspiracies and are

dismissed without improving the premise[8]. Propaganda does not represent the entire argument

and therefore does not rely on reality. Propaganda can be thought of as a "sixth sense" that

emancipates totalitarianism from observation and reality. Why is propagating ideology so

important? Does public support matter in a totalitarian state? According to the Prussian theorist,

Carl Von Clausewitz, the people and what they think, makes up one third of the trinity – his

famous paradigm that describes the phenomenon of war[9]. The passion that consumes the people

is a vital component to harness in war – even in a totalitarian state. Harnessing the passion of the

people keeps the trinity, along with the Army and the Government[10] in perfect balance.

Propaganda is the vehicle by which the totalitarians promote their messages; ideology is the

source of power for propaganda.

If propaganda relies on ideology as a source of power, can ideology therefore be a center

of gravity? At the operational and tactical levels of war, Army doctrine and Joint Publications

direct us to identify enemy centers of gravity as actual forces, political leaders, or, at the strategic

level of war, alliances or national will[11]. In a Fourth Generation war of ideologies, such as the one

we are in now, the center of gravity is the ideology itself.

Ethics

---

[7] Hannah Arendt, The Origins of Totalitarianism, (New York: Hartcourt Brace & Company, 1979, 470).

[8] Ibid. 471

[9] Carl Von Clausewitz, On War, Howard, Michael, and Paret, Peter, Eds., Trans., (New York: Everyman's, 1993) 101

[10] Ibid.

[11] Joint Publication 3-0 Joint Operations, accessed 25 February 2007 from www.dtic.mil/doctrine, IV 9-10.

According to Stanley Cunningham, in his book <u>The Idea of Propaganda: A Reconstruction,</u> propaganda is pseudo-information with an important philosophical shortfall. His book is reliant on epistemology and ethics; he concludes that propaganda as unethical. He argues that propaganda is inherently unethical because is exploits information, poses as knowledge, generates belief systems, skews perceptions and systematically disregards epistemic values[12]. He also sites (but disagrees with) a propaganda neutrality thesis[13]. The neutrality thesis puts the ethical onus on the propagandist – not propaganda itself. Sort of like the adage of: "guns don't kill people, people kill people". If the neutrality thesis is right then the ethical onus falls on the ideology, not the process of communicating it. Cunningham argues epistemologically that propaganda cannot be knowledge because of its selective use of truth and its ability to alter beliefs[14]. Academically, his argument is compelling but the practical application of the argument makes the philosophical definition irrelevant. Philosophical debates seeking consensus in understanding the concept of knowledge cannot even agree on the definition of "truth"[15]. In the larger sense, it seems folly to be epistemologically concerned with the use of information that seeks to change minds as compared with other mind-changing kinetic methods such as direct combat.

 <u>Propaganda Techniques</u> written by Henry Conserva is another interesting work on propaganda. Conserva's background is in education and debate. As a debating coach, he armed his team with a practical knowledge of propaganda. By educating his debate team on the techniques of propaganda, the team could develop better arguments against it[16]. Conserva defines propaganda as a "… *communication of a point of view, moral, amoral or immoral with the*

---

[12] Stanley Cunningham, <u>The Idea of Propaganda: A Reconstruction.</u> , (Westport, Connecticut: Praeger Publishers, 2002, 3-4)

[13] Ibid. 129-130

[14] Ibid. 97-98

[15] Wikipedia.com, *Truth*, available at: <u>http://en.wikipedia.org/wiki/Truth</u>

[16] Henry Conserva, <u>Propaganda Techniques,</u> (Bloomington Illinois: 1st Books Library,2003)

ultimate goal of the recipient of the view voluntarily accepting the propagandist's view."[17]

Conserva's views then are in keeping with JP 3-53 and Dictionary.com. He regards propaganda with certain neutrality but acknowledges that the intentional biases preclude it from being true information. He summarizes by explaining that propaganda causes the reader to suggest, imply and assume; propaganda discourages reflection, reason and understanding.[18] Propaganda is biased information that intendeds to persuade the recipient to accept the propagandist's views. Conserva proclaims that the natural enemy of propaganda is education. If propaganda is so flawed and educated people recognize it as so, then why is it effective?

According to Cunningham, propaganda is effective not only because it simplifies the information (making is indiscernible to the intellectually lazy) but also because we are absolutely inundated with the messages. There are so many propaganda messages, many appearing as information, the victim of propaganda has little time apply to finding the real truth[19]. Additionally, much propaganda appeals to the prejudices and pre-established attitudes of the recipient. In other words, propaganda tells the recipient what he wants to hear. Preconceived notions and culturally installed biases reinforce propaganda. Propaganda reinforces what we already believe and forms a "safety net" for our norms. It allows us to legitimize our beliefs and it verifies our values are correct. Propaganda allows the individual to think collectively, with safety in numbers[20]. Cunningham suggests that the victims of propaganda have complicity in propaganda. The propagandee is not an innocent victim; he develops an appetite for the emotionally charged messages and, with acceptance, becomes a willing participant in their own oppression.[21] Wartime propaganda feeds on emotions like hate, fear and patriotism – messages that support the individual's emotions can bolster the passion of the people. Propaganda of all

---

[17] Ibid. iii
[18] Cunningham, The Idea of Propaganda, 98.
[19] Ibid. 105-106.
[20] Ibid. 107.
[21] Ibid. 145.

sorts has become so prolific that it becomes difficult to discern where it is and where it is coming from.

Categories and techniques

Perhaps the most useful section of Stanley Cunningham's book is his categorization of propaganda. Chapter four of Cunningham's book explains the nine basic categories of propaganda: Agitation, Integration, White, Black, Disinformation, Bureaucratic, Counterpropaganda, Hate, and Deed[22].

- o **Agitation Propaganda** – A form of propaganda that calls attention to a social or political problem. Agitation propaganda uses a variety of emotional messages to generate outrage, fear or anger.
- o **Integration Propaganda** – A form of propaganda that calls for unity to a cause or group. Integration propaganda calls for people to join a movement.
- o **White Propaganda** – propaganda that uses facts and truthful messages in a persuasive manner. Although is relies on truth, it is presented in a biased manner.
- o **Black Propaganda** – the reverse of White Propaganda. Black propaganda relies on lies, or erroneous information.
- o **Disinformation** – information that is intentionally designed to be misleading. Disinformation is designed to propagate rumors and assumptions.
- o **Bureaucratic Propaganda** – the use of reports and statistics to convey a point of view. Bureaucratic propaganda masks itself as legitimate scientific findings.
- o **Counterpropaganda** – counteractive propaganda designed to nullify or reverse an opponent's propaganda message. Counterpropaganda inadvertently provides feedback to the original propagandist.
- o **Hate Propaganda** – a form of agitation propaganda that assigns blame for the problem on a person, race, or nationality. Perhaps the most prolific form of propaganda in the twentieth century. A major goal of hate propaganda is to demoralize the enemy.
- o **Propaganda of the Deed** – symbolic acts that rely on media attention to convey the message. Deeds follow the adage "actions speak louder than words". Through the use of video and photography, Deeds transcend language barriers.

These nine categories form an excellent baseline for identifying types of propaganda and, are helpful in deducting possible reasons behind the messages. Within each one of these categories, a technique of employment is used.

---

[22] Ibid. 66-71

Henry Conserva explains that propaganda is conveyed using seven techniques: Faulty

Logic, Diversion and Evasion, Appealing to Emotion, Falsehood and Trickery, Playing on

Human Behavioral Tendencies, Techniques of Style, and Techniques of Reason and Common

Sense.[23]

- o **Faulty Logic** – The use of simplifications, appeal to inappropriate authorities, condemning the origin, biased sampling and faulty analogies.
- o **Diversion and Evasion** – Ad hominem, accusing the accuser, satire, name calling, choosing a scapegoat, and fear of the wicked alternative.
- o **Appealing to Emotion** – Traditions, demand for special consideration, personification, and using "hot and cold" (overtly emotional) words.
- o **Falsehood and Trickery** – Quotes out of context, false dilemmas, exaggeration of consequences, appeal to ignorance, false urgency, and forgone conclusions
- o **Playing on Human Behavioral Tendencies** – Repetition, slogans, testimonials, using a bias, stimulating curiosity, and utopian or dystopian fantasies.
- o **Techniques of Style** – Shock, proverbs, emphasize one point, shotgun approach, and making statements that doesn't face rebuttal.
- o **Techniques of Reason and Common Sense** – Metaphors, "yes, but", portraying weaknesses as strengths, and use of famous quotes.

By utilizing both Cunningham's categories and Conserva's techniques, we can analyze

propaganda using common terms. Most examples of propaganda, past and present, are described

using these terms. Understanding the propaganda we encounter is an important element in

developing counterpropaganda and competing messages and themes.

Examples from the 20th Century wars – Western Culture

The 20th Century's wars introduced the element of propaganda by utilizing the global

media. During World War I, British, French, German and American all produced wartime

propaganda messages. Most were directed to their own populations with the intention of

informing or directing them to a cause (see appendix 1). Recruiting and resource preservation

were most common. Each side used satire and emotion to demonize the enemy while promoting

---

[23] Conserva, <u>Propaganda Techniques</u>.

their own. Interestingly, the civilian populations were the first to produce propaganda – not the governments[24]. Of all the communication mediums, none was more influential than the cinema. Charlie Chaplin starred in *Shoulder Arms* in 1918, a story that depicts Chaplin as a common recruit who single-handedly captures the Kaiser[25]. The movie is categorized as Integration Propaganda that uses Diversion (satire) as a technique. Perhaps it was created for entertainment but the effect was one of calling the allied audience together, united against the Germans. Charlie Chaplin's appearances in front of crowds boosted the sales of war bonds. By using comedy, it also relieved much of the fears of joining the Army thereby aided recruitment. There are weaknesses. The popular effect of the film could have been mitigated had the Germans been able to convey an alternative message showing the German soldier as a capable, ruthless killer rather than the bumbling fools as portrayed in *Shoulder Arms*. Of course, that alternative message would never have aired in the United States due to censorship[26]. Censorship is much less of a concern in today's realm of global communications.

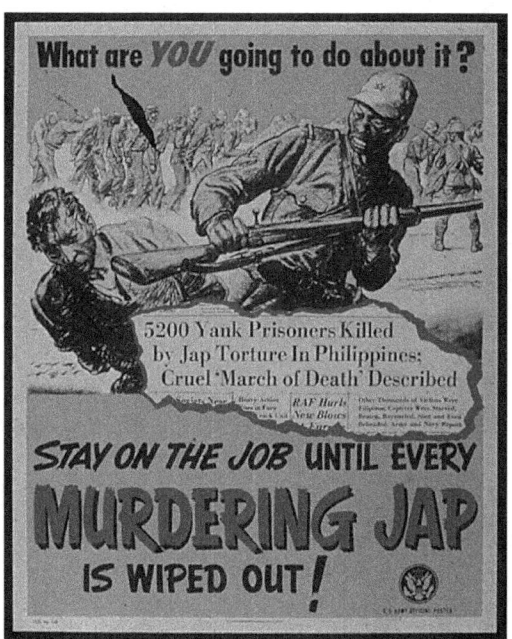

World War II was much larger than World War I in terms of battlefields and in terms of propaganda. Like the First World War, nations fighting in the 1930s and 1940s called upon their populations to work harder, produce more and consume less. Of course, there was always a call for recruitment (see appendix 2). World War II used the theme of racial hatred and fear to a much higher degree than in the previous world war. Viewing the propaganda posters of the period reveals

---

[24] Jay Winger and Blaine Baggett, <u>The Great War and the Shaping of the 20th Century</u>, (New York: Penguin Studio, 1996) 139.
[25] Ibid. 143
[26] Ibid.

more grotesque caricatures and more frightening images. In Figure 2, we see a Japanese soldier assaulting a helpless American prisoner. It also contains an excerpt from a newspaper describing the Bataan Death March. The poster is filled with propaganda messages. The poster falls into three separate categories: Agitation, drawing attention to the atrocities being committed by the Japanese; Integration, calling on the American workforce to stay on the job producing war materials; and Hate, identifying the atrocities with a race. The techniques of the poster are also well thought out. First, it appeals to emotion. Illustrated are the concern for America's soldiers and an appeal for revenge or justice. Secondly, the poster calls on human behavior; it calls on the population to solve the problem. Lastly, its style shocks the reader with its brutality then offers a way to "get even". There are weaknesses. A Japanese alternative message may have told a different point of view; American worker's efforts just line the big businessman's pockets with cash or another view that Japan's actions in the war were to counter America's imperialism in the Pacific. These messages (if attempted) never reached the American media because of censorship – no longer a significant barrier.

As in World War I, the cinema was decisive in spreading propaganda. Although the United States' Government contracted some of Hollywood's talents, the vast majority of films were produced privately. Movies varied from comedies like *Road to Morocco* with Bob Hope to dramas like *Guadalcanal Diary* with Anthony Quinn, and *Back to Bataan* with John Wayne[27]. The movies told stories to entertain the audience but also presented patriotic themes and messages where the American or British star was the hero and the Japanese or German was the evil villain. The influence of those films continues today. Every day in America, Memorial Day especially, countless classic World War II movies are broadcast on cable television communicating the themes and messages from over 60 years ago. To this day, World War II is commonly referred to a "The last good war". Hollywood continues to produce war movies about World War II – is that

---

[27] C.L. Sulzberger, The American Heritage Picture History of World War II, (New York: Random House, 1994) 476.

because it was indeed the last good war or is it because the propaganda of the time was so effective that it is widely accepted as such? Propaganda messages have a long shelf life.

Summary

In the simplest of terms, propaganda is deliberately biased information. It has a reputation for being constructed from lies, exaggerations, and falsehoods but it can be truthful. Because it intentionally omits known information, it is epistemologically unethical. Biased information, when recognized as such, is fairly harmless and generally neutral. The larger ethical problem is what *idea* or *ideology* the propagandist desires to convey. Wartime propaganda seeks to influence the recipients to support an idea or ideology. Totalitarian ideologies tend to be closed-minded and lack dialectic exchange. The lack of dialog supports the totalitarian leadership making them all-powerful in the minds of their people. Like propaganda itself, totalitarian governments are categorically unethical. Despite its ethical shortcomings, propaganda is prevalent in the modern global media and in Fourth Generation Warfare. Advertising, political messages, television programming and music are just a few forms of communication that covey messages with the intention of changing minds and attitudes. Propaganda is categorized by the effect it is designed to achieve such as integration, agitation or hate. Furthermore, propaganda uses some common techniques that play on emotion to convey the message to different sociological groups. The categories and techniques of propaganda evolved during the course of the 20th Century's world wars. When we analyze examples of propaganda using the categories and techniques we can discover weaknesses and inconsistencies that can aid in developing counter messages and themes. Countering a propaganda message in the 20th Century was difficult because of the effectiveness of censorship; in today's modern global media and communications network (and internet), it becomes nearly impossible to censor a rival's message. Education is the natural enemy of propaganda. The realm of global freedom of speech should be used to educate effected populations and thereby greatly weaken an opponent's propaganda. In a war of ideas like the Global War on Terrorism, the enemy's ideological weaknesses and inconsistencies should be identified and exploited.

THE CHINESE EXAMPLE

Propaganda changed during the Cold War and the later part of the 20th Century and Communist China used it effectively. Institutionalized propaganda in China was developed to be a holistic and all-encompassing form of information that masked indoctrination as education. Over a period of roughly 35 years from 1926 until 1960, propaganda successfully converted a huge population to support and accept an ideology based on the promise of a better life that would relieve the suffering masses from grips of capitalism. Its egalitarian style is similar to the current Jihadist ideology. Each ideology relies on the strength and equality of the masses over the international rule of law and each ideology promised(s) relief from the servitude imposed by the Western capitalist powers. During the 1950s, Chinese propaganda was incredibly successful but they had certain advantages that the Jihadists do not. While looking at the Chinese example, we will summarize the key points of Mao's ideology, review Mao's step-by-step strategy to gain control over Chinese society, and illustrate some of the methods and techniques used to shape the political structure of Communist China. The literature chosen as sources for Mao's ideology and the effects of his propaganda campaign were of the period. Invaluable sources for this chapter are Mao's own Selected Works, and two works from western authors: To Change a Nation by Franklin Houn and Brain-Washing in Red China by Edward Hunter. I used works from the period because they do not reflect the effects of history on the original propaganda messages. Contemporary sources on the Chinese Revolution tend to mitigate the power of the message through hindsight observations such as the failures of the "Great Leap Forward". Of the period sources recognized that the West was powerless to counter the Communist's propaganda due to China's closed society. That closed society prevented the people from hearing the ideas of democracy. This monograph chapter does not analyze the merits, detriments or ethical characteristics of Chinese Communism; instead, it focuses on the ideology's promotion and its acceptance in China.

The Ideology of Mao

In the Selected Works of Mao Tse-Tung, Volume One 1926 – 1936, Mao first describes a huge sociological problem that faces his country – the problem of imperialism[28]. Mao explains how the people of China do not have autonomy. Instead, they are ruled indirectly by the capitalist powers that control China's many warlords. The work of the peasants does not benefit their own society but instead benefits the imperialists. Without autonomy and self-rule, the Chinese would continue to work as slaves for a foreign power. Mao identifies the Kuomintang regime of China was a significant contributor to the problem. The regime, he says, "…*has capitulated to imperialism and at home replaced old warlords with new ones, and has subjected the working class and peasantry to an economic exploitation and political oppression even more ruthless than before.*"[29] Furthermore, Mao observed that since there were several imperialist powers indirectly controlling China, there would never be any unity of the Chinese people. On page 63 of volume one he writes "…*as long as China is divided up among the imperialist powers, the various cliques of warlords cannot under any circumstances come to a compromise …*" Without unity and autonomy, China could never control its own destiny; it would forever be ruled by foreign powers and never return to its great status it had for centuries. As a solution to this problem, Mao's ideology called to replace the imperialist power with the power and rule of the peasants. For this to happen, the peasantry would have to rise up and seize control over China.

Mao's ideology called for revolution to replace the imperialist-controlled, warlord-rule over China. This revolution was egalitarian in nature; it was communism. The solution Mao wrote was "…*China's democratic revolution…includes overthrowing the rule in China of*

---

[28] Mao Tse-Tung, Selected Works of Mao Tse-Tung, Volume One 1926 – 1936, (New York: International Publishers, 1954). 64
[29] Ibid. 63

imperialism and it tools, the warlords, so as to complete the national revolution; and carrying out

the agrarian revolution so as to eliminate the feudal exploitation of the peasants by the landed

gentry."[30] Mao's vision of a revolution promised a better life for the peasants under Chinese

communism. His vision included an eventual industrialization and collectivization of industry in

China. The revolution would be a change in all of Chinese society – not just politics but change in

culture, literacy, industry and governance. This vision was essential in propagating the ideology –

Mao would not be another warlord – with progress and modernization, he would deliver his

people from the grips of feudalism and put them in control. To gain the unified power of the

peasantry he would have to convince the populous that his ideas would do all that he promised.

During the war years, from the mid 1920s until the late 1940s, Mao led the Revolution unified

under the Communists. He overthrew the ruling government, and ousted the occupying Japanese.

His political work did not end there; his propaganda machine continued to persuade, convince

and compel the people of China to accept and follow the ideology for years to come. Mao's

strategy for dissemination for propaganda evolved from "word of mouth" as delivered by the Red

Army in the early years to all-encompassing inundation of totalitarian media control after 1949.[31]

Strategy of propagation

Mao's first obstacles to the success of the revolution were the existence of China's

aforementioned ruling government and the occupying Japanese. Ridding China of these rulers

was necessary to the revolution and would accomplish "phase one" but would not in itself install

the communist government. "Phase two" was leading Chinese society to the embodiment the

communist doctrine. To communicate with the Chinese people, the communists developed a

series of persistent themes and messages. This propaganda changed and adapted as the Chinese

Revolution matured. First themes addressed Chinese Nationalism and the evils of foreign

---

[30] Ibid. 64

[31] Franklin Houn, To Change a Nation: Propaganda and Indoctrination in Communist China, (New York: Crowell-Collier Publishing, 1961) 27-29.

imperialism. Mao's propaganda messages are categorized as *Agitation Propaganda* – messages that bring attention to a social problem. The next series of themes emphasized current events and successes of the party. This propaganda was disseminated in the Chinese controlled news and in the newly redeveloped schools. This category of propaganda was heavily laden with *Integration Propaganda, White Propaganda* and *Bureaucratic Propaganda*. Later propaganda themes and messages challenged the traditional agrarian society to become an industrial society. This theme was propagated in the compiled outlets of news, schools, radio, printed art and performing arts and entertainment. Mao's challenge was the chronic underdevelopment of China. Obstacles to overcome in the quest of propagating the political message of the Revolution were Chinese peasant illiteracy, inadequate print media, lack of significant radio broadcasting and radios for the public and non-political arts and entertainment. Mao lacked the resources to overcome all obstacles simultaneously but the one resource he could count on was the Red Army.

The Red Army

For Mao, fighting was not a military task alone. In the chapter of *Rectification of Incorrect Ideas in Party*, from the Selected Works, Mao explains that the military must carry out the leading political work in addition to destroying the enemy's military might. The Red Army's tasks in achieving independence included such tasks as "…*agitating the masses, organizing them, arming them and helping them to set up revolutionary political power and even establishing organizations of the Communist Party.*"

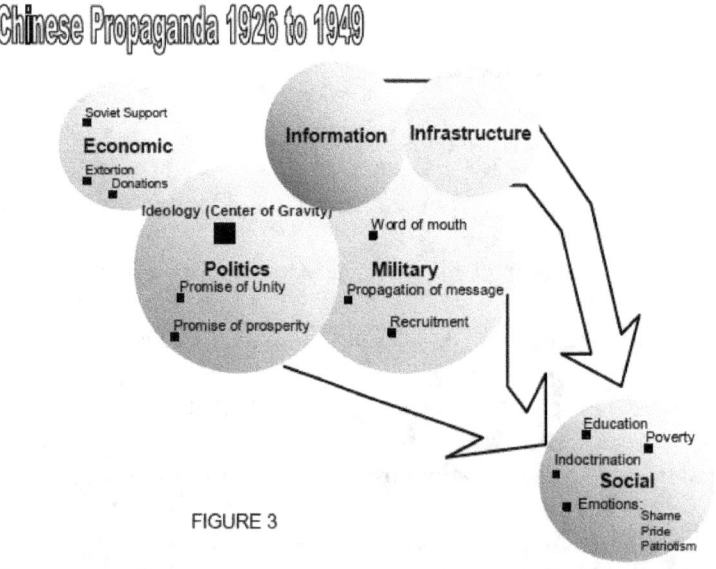

FIGURE 3

He goes on to explain that the Red Army loses its reason for existence if it cannot propagate the political ideology[32]. During the early years of the Revolution, Mao used the Red Army to target both the Kuomintang regime and the Japanese occupiers with both kinetic and non-kinetic (i.e. political) effects. In his Selected Works, Volume Three, Mao explains how the communist party and the Red Army must not neglect the political work with the Chinese peasants to combat the Japanese Army. The success of the Chinese Revolution relied on the cumulative effects of the Red Army and the Communist Party working together. They were careful to include all of the Chinese society. From their established bases in the rural areas, the Red Army and the Communist Party could exercise an open existence with the peasantry. In cities where the enemy forces were powerful, they hid their existence but exercised guerilla warfare and propaganda. [33] The close cooperation between the Red Army and the Communist Party didn't end with the Revolution. Even today, the Chinese soldier is thoroughly indoctrinated with political thought. During a discussion with Colonel Hu[34], Chinese visitor to the Combined Arms Center, Fort Leavenworth, I was informed that Chinese soldiers continue to undergo political education to correctly understand the values of Chinese ideology as well as the policies of the Chinese Government. Their political education begins during initial training and continues periodically throughout their time in service. A Chinese Army soldier is expected to be able to communicate the politics of the state. Mao's legacy in the Chinese Army continues – the soldier and the political message are inseparable.

By the early 1950s, the Communist Party could begin to rely on government officials to communicate propaganda. The Red Army's services shifted away from the homeland and to the Korean peninsula. However, the revolution in China was not complete – not until the communist

---

[32] Mao, Selected Works Vol. One. 106

[33] Mao Tse-Tung, The Selected Works of Mao Tse-Tung, Volume Three 1939-1941, (New York: International Publishers, 1954) 84-86.

[34] Colonel Hu visited the Combined Arms Center at Fort Leavenworth Kansas. I spoke to him as part of a visiting Chinese delegation on 5 December, 2006.

ideology was firmly set in Chinese society. Mao's government created a new branch in the government that Franklin Houn refers to as the "propaganda army of the party"[35]. Education, literacy and the media were still far from developed so the Chinese government once again relied on word of mouth propaganda. The propaganda army of the party created Propaganda Officers, Reporting Officers, and non-party helpers to continue the indoctrination of the country. The propaganda officer was usually a community leader working in a collective farm, factory or other massive organization. He attended communist seminars and classes where he became an expert in the ideology. His task was to teach the ideology to his friends and coworkers. Propaganda officers took on this role as an additional duty to their regular labor positions. It was important that these teachers of communism were egalitarian and seen as one of the people rather than some far-removed government official. By 1952 there were nearly 3 million propaganda officers working in China. The propaganda army also created a position called the Reporting Officer. The reporting officer was higher in rank than the propaganda officer was. The reporting officer had the responsibility of maintaining the statistics and filing reports regarding the successes of the party and the country's shift to communism[36]. The institutional structure of Mao's China is not yet possible in the Jihadist movement; the Jihadists lack the kind of effective government Mao used to consolidate his political gains.

Education and Literacy

To realize industrialization and collectivization, China would have to learn to read and write. This was a signification problem as only 20 percent of China's population was literate.[37] From the birth of the revolution, through the war years and into the 1950s, the communists sought to educate the public – reading, writing and the theories of communism. Before mass education could become a reality, the communists had to gain control over the intellectuals in society. In

---

[35] Houn, 45-53
[36] Ibid. 48-49
[37] Houn., 28.

Chinese culture, it was not uncommon for the intellectuals to actively participate in political

activities. When the Chinese Revolution gained momentum, many scholars were already familiar

with the theories of Marx, Lenin, and Mao. The communists selected and appointed scholars to

lead the war against ignorance. By 1957, the communists had all but wiped out illiteracy – over

65 percent of the population had achieved the ability to read and write[38]. Communist-run schools

sprang up all over communist China. In 1949, there were just over 24 million elementary schools;

in 1959, there were over 86 million. [39] All students improved their skills of reading and writing

but that was of no benefit to the party if they did not also receive education in communist theory.

The Chinese government experienced significant challenges with creating so many

schools. Where there were no schools, communist party officers lead "Study Groups" where

students met with teachers and studied at home (if literate) or attended lectures[40]. The schools

were an essential element in the indoctrination of the people but in some cases, they had no

teachers or textbooks. The demand for teachers drastically overwhelmed supply, which was a concern for the communist government. The government revised school curriculum to focus on patriotism and labor over history and

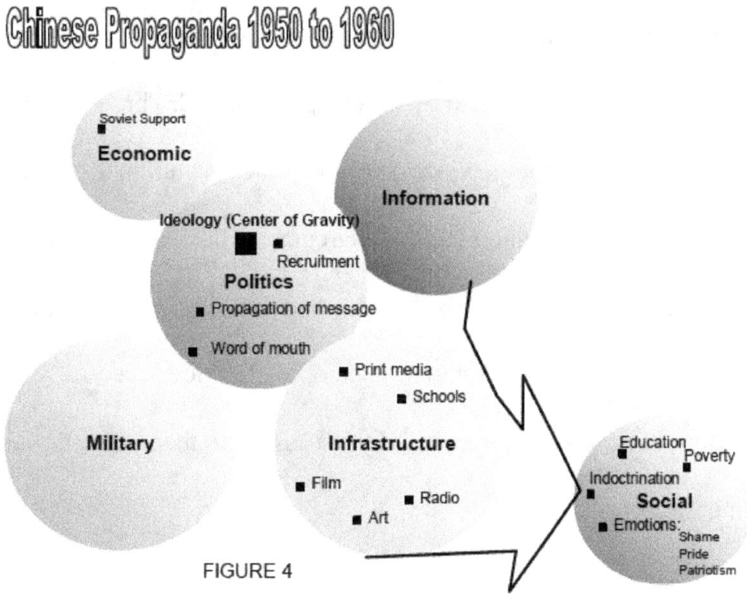

Chinese Propaganda 1950 to 1960

Soviet Support
Economic

Information

Ideology (Center of Gravity)
Recruitment
Politics
Propagation of message
Word of mouth

Print media
Schools

Military

Infrastructure

Education
Poverty
Indoctrination
Social
Emotions:
Shame
Pride
Patriotism

Film
Radio
Art

FIGURE 4

geography. Teachers were directed to emphasize the present rather than the past. The "political

---

[38] Ibid. 29-30, 38
[39] Ibid. 40
[40] Ibid. 41

reliability" of the teachers was suspect – there had not been enough time to properly screen and train teachers in the ways of communism. The lack of textbooks only exasperated the problem. All school textbooks were banned in 1949 and the recreation of a new library of politically reliable textbooks was a daunting task[41]. The Chinese government was the source of all education – competing thought and Western ideology (demonized as imperialism) had little chance of reversing the tide of communism in that closed society. This control over education by the Chinese government is a classic example of *Bureaucratic Propaganda* as described by Cunningham[42]. The Jihadists lack this ability. They will continue to struggle against uncensored education in our globalized world.

Modernization of the Chinese Media

Education of the masses was supplemented with a growing, communist-controlled Chinese media. The Chinese government gained control of all news outlets, printing presses, radio broadcasting, stage productions and film. News about the revolution, as written by the communists, was disseminated by newspapers and radio broadcasting. The Chinese public regularly received "good news stories" about the revolution along with Chairman Mao's personal statements, comments, interviews and circulars. This intentionally biased information reached the public who received it as "news". Mao recognized the importance news stories but also paid a great deal of attention to Chinese art and culture. Mao successfully infused communist ideology with Chinese culture and propagated the message to the people through control of China's mass communications.

The earliest media outlet was created in the Soviet Union in 1932. The news service was called the Red China News Agency and it produced newspapers and radio broadcasts. Its purpose was to inform the population of China of the advancements of Chinese Communism in war and in

---

[41] Ibid. 75
[42] See chapter one

politics. In 1937 it was renamed the New China News Agency and began growing to meet the

needs of the Chinese Revolution – those needs of course was propaganda. By the late 1950s, the

New China News Agency was responsible for providing approved news stories to all Chinese

media outlets including newspapers, local, regional and international radio broadcasting. Local

news publications would commonly publish local news and information but the New China News

Agency provided all the leading national and international news.[43]. Mao personally provided

much of the material for the New China News Agency to disseminate. In his Selected Works, we

see many examples of Mao's written circulars, and other forms of correspondence. One such

example is in Volume Five, the period covering 1945 to 1949. China was in conflict with the

United States; the American government supported Chang Kai-Shek and the anti-communist

opposition. Mao conducted an interview with an American journalist named Anna Louise Strong.

During the interview, whose text was printed in Volume Five, Mao gave a political soliloquy

denouncing America's imperialism and praising China's bravery in the face of the "paper tiger".

In the text of the interview, Ms Strong seems to cooperate with Mao and his political philosophy

by asking pre-designed questions that Mao wanted to answer. The questions asked appeared to

give the piece a news-type quality. There was a large emphasis on the fact that the interviewer

was an American, which provides legitimacy to the interview[44]. Information on Anna Louise

Strong suggests she was anything but an objective journalist. It is true that she was an American

citizen and journalist but she also was pretty devout communist who was arrested on espionage

charges after World War II. She was a personal friend of Mao Tse-Tung and lived in China until

her death in 1970[45]. This example of propaganda is categorized as *White Propaganda* as

---

[43] Houn, 97-98.

[44] Mao Tse-Tung, The Selected Works of Mao Tse-Tung, Volume Five 1945-1949, (New York: International Publishers, 1954) 97-101.

[45] Reference Writers: Anna Louise Strong, accessed 15 December, 2007 from site: http://www.marxists.org/glossary/people/s/t htm#strong-anna-louise

described by Cunningham and delivered in technique that plays on *Human Behavior* (appeal to authority and emphasizing credentials) as described by Henry Conserva[46]

In a largely illiterate, underdeveloped society, communist newspapers and circulars were somewhat ineffective. Mao compensated for this shortcoming by directing villages, factories, schools, collective farms and military units to establish a daily meeting where one party member could read the newspaper to all the others. The location of the meeting became routine – mimeographed or blackboard news items were posted for collective use. Over time, the community news area became regular meeting place that served as an outlet for propaganda. The Chinese people routinely gathered for collective radio listening. By the early 1950s, radio broadcasts exposed propaganda and entertainment to larger numbers of Chinese[47].

The Communist regime began organized collective radio listening in 1951. At the time there were few Chinese radio broadcasting stations and a woefully inadequate numbers of radios for the public. Mao pushed for the development of radio as a means of modernization and as an effective way to communicate the ideology to the public. Mao compensated for the lack of radios by establishing community-owned radios complete with a system of loud speakers. Speakers were positioned in key public areas to include factories and other places of work. To ensure the public understood the broadcasts, Mao created Radio Monitoring Teams. They were responsible for assembling the public for selected broadcasts and, on occasion, summarize what the message meant. Over the next few years, the communist government established loud speakers on street corners, markets, places of work and nearly all public places. Programming increased too – between 1950 and 1955 radio broadcasts began around 06:45 and concluded around 20:45. Daily programming was divided by content; roughly 50 percent was news, and political in nature, 25 percent was social education and the last 25 percent was cultural and entertainment[48]. Despite the

---

[46] See chapter one.
[47] Houn, 127,161
[48] Ibid. 160-170.

technological advancements in Chinese broadcasting and overcoming the scarcity of radios the

communist government had one tragic flaw with radio – it became terribly boring. Mao's next

challenge was to make his message entertaining.

China had long had a rich culture complete with performing arts. Of all the traditional

art forms, perhaps the opera was China's most enjoyed. The communists could not allow

unrestricted performances – the fear being an expression of something anti-revolutionary. Starting

in 1945, Chinese performers were required to attend special political classes where they

underwent training and heard political speeches. In 1954, there were some 2,300 professional

opera companies with about 150,000 performers. There were 1,740 opera theaters but the opera

companies routinely performed wherever there were large gatherings of Chinese people. Opera

companies performed in factories, collective farms and at military camps[49]. The content of the

performances was controlled by the Ministry of Culture. Mao recognized the power of the

performer and demanded "politics be united with art."[50] The Ministry of Culture was tasked with

controlling China's Central Drama School. Traditional scripts were rewritten. One such example

was "Su San the Courtesan". The original version takes place during the Ming Dynasty. Su San is

a prostitute who falls in love with a young man. The young man desires to go to school and get an

education but he has no money. Su San pays for his education then waits for him to return. Since

she refuses to entertain any more men, she is sold into slavery. In her new home, she is accused of

murdering her master. Her master's wife committed the crime but bribed the local judge; Su San

is tortured into confessing to the crime. During her trial, the Young man, whom she sent to

school, appears as her attorney. He successfully defends his lover and the real criminals are

brought to justice. The Ministry of Culture altered this classic Chinese story so that the characters

would spend their time explaining the detriments of pre-revolutionary society and condemn such

---

[49] Ibid. 183-184.
[50] Edward Hunter, <u>Brain Washing in Red China, the Calculated Destruction of Men's Minds</u>,
(New York: The Vanguard Press, 1951) 308.

actions as social classes, prostitution and corruption. The whole opera becomes a lesson in communist values[51].

The Ministry of Culture also had a great effect on printed art. Artists and cartoonists were, like stage actors, required to understand communism and were taught how to convey political messages visually. The communists increased publications and produced politically inspired comic books. Printed art communicated to the literate and illiterate alike. Cartoons also communicated to the Chinese youth[52]. Illustrations conveyed many symbols – some obvious and some subliminal (see annex 3). Revolutionary soldiers can appear powerful and united in pursuit of communism, in other words, good role models. Likewise, propaganda posters conveyed political messages and promoted new policies to the Chinese people. The artwork depicts themes like patriotism, health, bounty, success, happiness and modernization in an effort to distract the public from inadequacies of the Great Leap Forward[53].

Summary

In the period of time between 1926 and 1960, Mao Tse-Tung changed China. It was a change that transformed China from a colonized, underdeveloped backward nation to a unified nation under communism. It started with Mao's Ideology. Mao had a vision of Chinese Communism; an egalitarian movement that would alleviate his people's suffering and restore China to its former glory. To realize his vision for China, Mao developed a military and propaganda strategy that would first free his country from Japanese imperialism then overthrow the existing Chinese government in revolution. Next, Mao would challenge China's traditional agrarian society and replace it with a modern industrialized society. Mao realized that politics and war were inseparable. The Red Army was created to fight for the cause in both the physical and

---

[51] Houn, 186 – 188.
[52] Hunter, 206 - 210
[53] Chinese propaganda posters and commentary downloaded 15 February 2007 from site: http://www.iisg.nl/exhibitions/chairman/chn01.php

political sense – it was the voice of the movement. In the early years, the Chinese Red Army was the primary means of communicating the message of communism to the people of China. They gained momentum in the rural regions where they had access to the peasantry. Mao's ideological war did not end with military victory over Chang Kai-Shek – the propaganda war to win the minds of the people continued. Education of the masses was necessary to disseminate the doctrine and to modernize China. Mao begun the Herculean task of bringing literacy to the millions of Chinese peasants who had never known how to read or write. Mao realized that the revolution was still fragile and that uncontrolled or unrestricted education may lead to the failure of Chinese communism. To compensate, Mao took control of the nation's education system. Pre-revolutionary textbooks were removed and teachers were screened for "political reliability" With his control over education, Mao was able to indoctrinate his people while simultaneously teaching them to read and write. Mao took control over the nation's newspapers and provided their newly educated population with reading material while denying them access to the outside world. Propaganda replaced information in the form of "News". China's growing broadcasting capability supplemented the printed media and great strives were made to entice the Chinese people to listen. Enticement meant improving the stuffy, boring political programming replacing it with classic – but politically altered – forms of Chinese art and theater. As the movement progressed, the communist government of China became the all-inclusive source for communications for her people.

THE JIHADIST'S EXAMPLE

Like Chinese Communism in the mid 20th Century, the Islamic Jihadists use propaganda to communicate the political message of their cause. The Jihadist movement shares some similarities with the communist movement: both are egalitarian, both seek to save their people from the ravages of Western imperialism, both have an ideology that promises to restore greatness to their respective cultures. There are, however, several key differences, differences that make the Jihadist movement more vulnerable as compared with Chinese communism. The

Jihadist movement is based on a religion – one that is widely interpreted; the Jihadists do not

have one clear leader – their movement lacks unity of effort and a wide variety of actions

contradict the ideology. Most importantly, the Jihadist movement is competing for the minds of

the people in an open society where free press and free speech (through globalization) are

unavoidable. There are several invaluable resources to explore when understanding Jihadist

ideology. Perhaps the most invaluable is <u>Milestones</u> by Seyyid Qutb. <u>Milestones </u>is the first

modern work sited as a source for Islamic ideology. Stemming from Qutb is a more contemporary

manuscript entitled <u>The Management of Savagery</u> translated by Doctor Will McCants of the

Combating Terrorism Center at West Point. This is an especially important work as it serves as

doctrine for the Jihadist's war on America. Lastly, a panel of terrorism experts provided a current

analysis and in depth understanding of Jihadist propaganda. The presentation included a

discussion of images, themes and translated messages downloaded from the internet. This chapter

will discuss the Jihadist ideology, their strategy for propagation, the use of military forces, the

problems with literacy and the use of the media. This monograph chapter does not analyze the

merits, detriments or ethical characteristics of Islamic ideology; instead, it focuses on the

ideology's promotion and its acceptance in the Muslim world.

The Jihadist Ideology

The Jihadist ideology is similar to the ideology Mao used to unify China in that both

identify Western imperialism as a primary cause for suffering. The current problems of

"backwardness", subjugation, colonialism and general weakness of the nation of Islam have

troubled Muslims for some time. In his book <u>Islam: The Straight Path</u>, John Esposito explains

that modern Muslim leaders have struggled with the western powers since the 18th Century. In a

cultural movement known as Islamic Revivalism, which began with the Wahhabist movement in

18th Century Arabia, caused Islamic leaders to deduce that their people suffer at the hands of the western powers because Muslims have displeased God. By the 18th Century, Imperial Islam was in serious decline. World power had shifted from the Middle East to Europe. The West's superiority in science, technology and economic prosperity soon overcame the influences of the Muslims. The revivalists believed that the temptations of western cultural led Muslims away from the "straight path" and enticed them to engage in less traditional behavior as dictated in the Hadith and the Shariah[54]. They believed Muslims had foregone Muhammad's example for the lust of material idol worship as demonstrated in western capitalist societies. Because of this disobedience, God has punished Muslims with weakness. Revivalists believed that greatness could only be restored by returning to the ways of the Prophet[55].

The European powers and influence over the Middle East only grew during the 19th and 20th Centuries. By 1920, even the once great Ottoman Empire had collapsed. The European powers of Brittan and France, victors over the Ottomans in World War I, had taken much of the Middle East as colonies[56]. Islamic Modernists sought to combat European encroachment by reexamining Islam and reform Islamic ways to compete with the West. Such reforms would drastically increase efforts at education. To the Islamic Modernists, mastering science and technology was required to keep up with the contemporary times. When Modernists abdicated political reforms, such as adopting secular government, a crisis developed within Islamic society. From this crisis developed revivalist organizations like the Muslim Brotherhood.[57]. Effectively, there was a split in the Nation of Islam: Revivalists desired national unity and a restoration to preeminence through devote adherence to traditional Islamic law and a return to the ways of the Prophet; Modernists desired national unity and a restoration to preeminence through education, science, technology and – if necessary – secularism. Secularism was not an attractive option for

---

[54] Hadith is a narrative report of the Prophet Muhammad's sayings and actions; Shariah is Islamic law based on the Hadith – see glossary of Esposito.

[55] John L. Esposito, Islam: The Straight Path, Third Edition, (New York, Oxford: Oxford University Press, 2005) 115-119, 165.

[56] David Fromkin, Peace to End All Peace, (New York: Henry Holt and Company, 1989) Maps between pages 20 – 21.

[57] Esposito, 125 - 127

either group. Even the modernists viewed the West's secular governments as morally bankrupt[58].

Compromise between the two factions, such as secular administrative law combined with Islamic

family law, quieted the rift for a time but neither side was satisfied and preeminence has yet to be

realized.

Later in the 20th Century the ideas of the revivalists was renewed and a group Esposito

now refers to as the Neorevivalists have made their views known. A resurgence of the Muslim

Brotherhood and member-authors like Seyyid Qutb became especially powerful religious

societies with political power. Theirs was a position abdicating complete independence from the

West sighting a self-sufficiency of Islamic society through devote piety. Meanwhile, several

Islamic societies began to emulate the Western culture and adopted many nontraditional lifestyles

such as Western dress, music, movies, politics etc. Neorevivalists could accept neither capitalism

nor Marxism. Each was demonic in its own way. To groups like the Muslim Brotherhood, Islam

and the Shariah was the only way of life – all other cultures and societies live in perpetual sin and

darkness. By 1949, the Neorevivalists resorted to violence when Egypt failed to become an

Islamic state[59].

Qutb's writings are considered by experts[60] to be a founding document for the militant

Neorevivalists to include Osama Bin Laden. It is accurate to assess Milestones as anti-American

and anti-Western however, Qutb concentrates his philosophy on the power of Islam and the

importance of following the Shariah as it was written some fourteen-hundred years ago.

Throughout the work, specifically chapters 2, 3 and 6, Qutb stresses that law devised by man is

inherently sinful – there is no way to avoid it. Man without God is an animal; laws made by

animals only serve worldly goals such as food, shelter and sex[61]. God's laws are perfect and

---

[58] Ibid.

[59] Ibid. 149, 151, 153

[60] LDR Youssef Aboul-Enein, *Sheikh Abdel-Fatah Al-Khalidi Revitalizes Sayid Qutb*, accessed 1 March, 2007 from site: http://www.ctc.usma.edu/Khalidi-Qutb3.pdf

[61] Seyyid Qutb, Milestones, (Dar Al-Ilm, Damascus, Syria 1960?) 51

universal - all of mankind will benefit when they submit to them. Additionally, God is sovereign over man; if God is sovereign, how can man create any law that is contradictory? Qutb calls for Muslims to fight for freedom under the Shariah (mankind would not suffer from war, poverty and famine under God's laws – this is his concept of freedom). Qutb's ideology is utopian. He stresses that only a strict Islamic state is one where God is the sovereign, the Quran is the constitution and the Shariah is the law, can avoid the sinful existence of Jahiliyyah – or life devoid of divine guidance[62]. There is, of course, no state that meets this "Shariah Only" criterion.

Despite his distain for modern governments, including Muslim heads of state, Qutb does not overtly call for violence to achieve his utopian vision. He recognizes universal acceptance of Islam will take time. Meanwhile, life on earth requires Islamic people to live at peace with the Jahiliyyah societies without adopting their un-Islamic ways. In chapter 10 Qutb explains that the Muslim must demonstrate piety and superiority of faith while offering a bridge to Jahiliyyah people – a bridge for them to cross over and join the blessings of Islam[63]. Qutb's work is not without reference to Jihad. In chapter 4, Qutb explains that Jihad should be fought to allow a person the choice to become Muslim. He says that only God can create a Muslim. Jihad is fought so that tyrannical men, whose oppression has denied God's law, are forced to remove the manufactured barriers of the faith. Perhaps it is this chapter that inspired Osama Bin Laden.

In 1996, Osama Bin Laden issued his fatwa declaring war against the United States. The logic of this declaration is that the Islamic Nation cannot be revived because the United States prevents it. Removing the United States from the Islamic world will allow Islam to flourish, and regain is once known grandeur. This declaration modified the neorevivalist ideology into the current Global Jihadist ideology we confront today. Bin Laden's statement in 1996 calls for an end to passive resistance against the West – particularly the United States. He references the lack of Shariah law in Saudi Arabia as a grievance but the preponderance accusations against America

---

[62] Ibid Ch 9-10.
[63] Ibid 140.

has to do with the regional economy, national wealth and oil. Bin Laden calls for a universal Islamic Jihad to punish America for a long list of grievances, everything from walking on the soil of Arabia to the killing of Iraqis, to supporting Israel and the Saudi regime. The long, and sometimes incoherent tirade, makes it difficult to ascertain the actual purpose for the Jihad. It is different than the previous ideological works of the revivalists or modernists in that Bin Laden does not seek the advancement of Islam but only seeks to punish the United States[64]. Bin Laden issued another fatwa in 1998. This message was much shorter than his 1996 statement and followed a narrower focus. The '98 message has no reference to Shariah law. It only calls upon Muslims to wage Jihad out of hatred for America – not the advancement of Islam[65]. The fatwas' publications not only update (and weaken) the neorevivalist ideology but their emotional tones and over-simplifications of complex social issues, allow the messages to serve as propaganda.

Strategy of Propagation

The current Jihadist movement lacks unity of command and proceeds only because of consensus and popularity. The ideology, based on the sovereignty of God over man, makes it difficult for any one person to lead the movement. Osama Bin Laden's fatwas and actions against the United States temporarily unified the Jihadists but not in a hierarchal fashion; the unification is more like moral support for common thinkers. Because of their declaration of war and their sensational terrorist strikes against the United States, the Al Qaeda Network has, by default, become an ideological leader in the Global Jihad. Osama Bin Laden, a "Jihadist Robin Hood", must rely on popularity to lead. The Al Qaeda Network maintains its loose leadership by maintaining the regional mood – one that is anti-western and especially anti-American. They must maintain the emotional tide of the Islamic world. Their use of propaganda is unconventional

---

[64] *Bin Laden's Fatwa*, Online News Hour, accessed 1 March 2007 from site: http://www.pbs.org/newshour/terrorism/international/fatwa_1996.html
[65] *Al Qaeda's Fatwa*, Online News Hour, accessed 1 March 2007 from site: http://www.pbs.org/newshour/terrorism/international/fatwa_1998.html

but not asymmetric. They cannot propagate the ideology the way Mao did in 20th Century China. Theirs is a more difficult task since they do not control any country, the do not have a force the size of the Red Army to forcibly spread the ideology, nor can they control the schools throughout the Middle East. The Islamists cannot control any of the media but, unlike Mao, have found a way to use the global media network to do their work for them. By using their military forces to conduct sensational terrorist attacks on the hated Americans, the Jihadists can rely on our own media to show the images, and the message, to the world. Attacking and hurting the

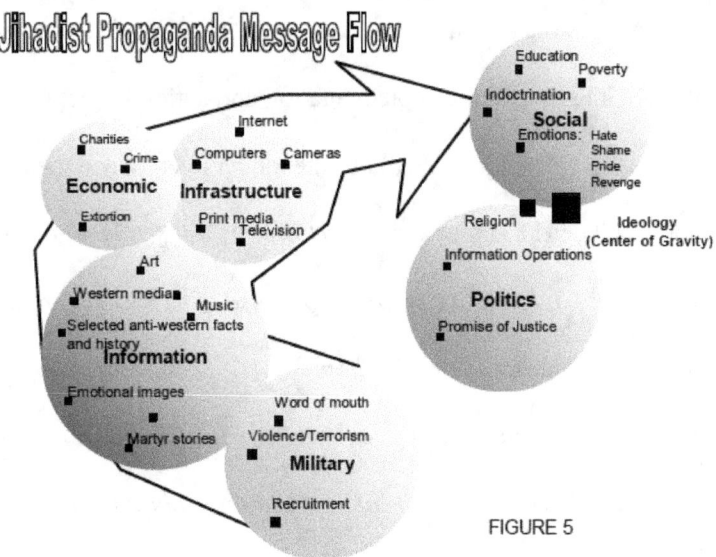

FIGURE 5

enemy brings popularity and support to the cause. In this way, Maneuver actually supports Information Operations, not the other way around – a characteristic of Fourth Generation Warfare. Figure 5 shows how violence and terrorism create information that is disseminated through the infrastructure (international media, internet, satellite television, etc.) that influence the social system that in turn maintains the political system. Without popularity, Al Qaeda cannot raise money, recruit, or propagate the ideology. Popularity is vital and is developed though the combination of *Propaganda of the Deed*, *Agitation Propaganda* and *Integration Propaganda*.

The Jihadist Military Forces

Propaganda of the Deed, as described by Cunningham, is communicating a message with action. Cunningham illustrates deed propaganda with peaceful examples such as sit-ins, marches and even saluting. He believes that terrorism is too extreme to be propaganda[66] but, as explained in the <u>Management of Savagery</u>, it serves the purpose of communication. What Cunningham refers to as terrorism, the Jihadists refer to as military action. <u>The Management of Savagery</u>, as described by Doctor Will McCants a Fellow of the Combating Terrorism Center at West Point, is a type of "doctrine" for the Jihadists[67]. According to McCants, this doctrine was written for "middle management" leaders in the Jihad. The document connects the Jihadist ideology with strategy for implementation and action in the war against America. The Jihadists recognize that their fighters will use the media to convey a message to the world – enemy and supporter alike. The author writes: *"However, if it sends all of its members on this secure (by the permission of God) operation for the purpose of massacring and terrorizing the enemy, when the people and the newspapers talk about what happened, the people and the enemy will think that the coming operations will be even more concentrated and have a commensurate numerical increase, which will raise the reputation of the mujahids in the media and dissuade the hearts from opposing them."*[68] Here the Jihadists rely on the media to communicate propaganda – the message, as communicated through terrorist attacks. This propaganda seeks to raise the reputation and prestige of the forces in the cause. Additionally, military forces are used to gain access to the media in order to communicate: *"For example, we kidnap a hostage and then provoke a large outcry over them and demand that the television reporters and the media networks announce what we want to say in full to the people in exchange for handing over the hostages"*[69]. Here again the Jihadists use military actions to convey political messages through the use of our media.

The war in Iraq is full of examples of the militant forces conducting deed propaganda. This type of propaganda is decisive to the Jihadist strategy. The strategy, as described in Osama

---

[66] Cunningham, 71

[67] Interview with Dr Will McCants conducted in conjunction with a panel discussion on Inside the Mind of a Terrorist. Panel and interview conducted 26 October, 2006.

[68] <u>The Management of Savagery</u>, translated by Dr Will McCants, (John M. Olin Institute for Strategic Studies, Harvard University, 23 May, 2006) 29 of the original text

[69] Ibid. 42

Bin Laden's 1996 Fawta[70], is to attack the will of American public by causing casualties.

Casualties and the general unpleasantness of war will compel America to leave the Middle East.

Insurgents and Jihadists seek the cumulative propaganda effect of casualties. There are

comparatively few examples of purely military aims in the actions of the insurgent forces. As

listed on the *Multi National Forces Iraq* web site, terrorist attacks consist primarily of bombings,

assassinations, kidnappings and sabotage[71]. These actions fail to achieve significant military

effects at the tactical level but communicate messages cumulatively through the media at the

strategic level. The constant and persistent level of violence communicates an inability of the

coalition forces to win in Iraq. Casualties inflicted on coalition forces achieve no tactical purpose;

all casualties are inflicted to support the propaganda strategy of the Jihadists. If a picture is worth

a thousand words then an American causality is worth a thousand pictures. As stated before,

Maneuver supports Information Operations in Fourth Generation Warfare.

Education and Literacy

Neorevivalists require intellectuals and politicians adopt science, technology and

government studies from the Quran rather than from intellectual dialog with the West[72]. There is

a similarity here between Mao and the Neorevivalists – both wish to isolate their intelligentsia

from the West. The problem for the Islamic world in the late 20th Century was that the West had

the predominance of educational resources and it was not based on the Quran. After the Soviet

Union invaded Afghanistan, Saudi Arabia began to fund Islamic schools known as Madrassas –

an outlet for *Bureaucratic Propaganda*. Madrassas were born during the Jihad against the Soviet

Union to educate its students in military arts as well as Islam. The student's demographic was

typically that of poor or impoverished Islamic society – perhaps the best suited for ideological

---

[70] *Bin Laden'a Fawta 1996*

[71] *Terrorist Tactics*, Operation Iraqi Freedom accessed 3 March 2007 from site: http://www.mnf-iraq.com/index.php?option=com_content&task=view&id=727&Itemid=44

[72] Esposito, 152

indoctrination. Most of the schools were established in the region around Pakistan and

Afghanistan – close to the source of Mujahideen fighters. After the defeat of the Soviet Union,

the madrassas continued to flourish. With the absence of the Soviets, they have changed targets to

the Americans[73]. The Jihadist movement discourages intellectuals from conversing with the West

and it seeks to limit education outside of the Quran. Recently in Iraq, there was an attack on

Baghdad's Book Market. The Book Market is an urban scene where intellectuals gather, play

backgammon and talk politics. Books are exchanged and discussions expand into science,

technology, government and politics. Tragically on 6 March 2007, the market was bombed.

According to a report published by the New York Times, an Iraqi poet and frequent visitor said,

"There are no Americans or Iraqi politicians here — there are only Iraqi intellectuals who

represent themselves and their homeland, plus stationery and book dealers… Those who did this

are like savage machines intent on harvesting souls and killing all bright minds."[74] An attack

such as this serves more than one purpose – on the surface it discourages others from involving

themselves with non-Islamic study; below the surface, it is the act itself that is supposed to teach.

This attack is what the Jihadists call "Education by Momentous Event", a form of *Propaganda by*

the Deed.

In section 10 of <u>The Management of Savagery</u>, the author describes the importance of

education within the movement. He does not discuss education in terms of literacy, science or

technology but instead concentrates on the communication of the religion and ideology in a

Quranic tradition. Listed is what the author calls "Methods of Education". Methods of Education

are: *Education by Exhortation (stories), Education by Habit, Education by Pious Deed,*

Education by Example, and *Education by Momentous Events.* Of these categories, Education by

Momentous Events and Education by Example are the most important. Momentous Events, like

---

[73] *Analysis Madrassas,* <u>PBS Front Line</u>, accessed 7 March 2007 from site:
http://www.pbs.org/wgbh/pages/frontline/shows/saudi/analyses/madrassas.html
[74] *Middle East Section,* <u>New York Times</u> accessed 6 March, 2007 from site:
http://www.nytimes.com/2007/03/06/world/middleeast/06cnd-troops.html?_r=1&hp&oref=slogin

the terrorist attacks on 9/11 *"capture the peoples' attention and which the mujahid movement endures, and the steadfastness of human exemplars in the face of horrors resulting from these events firmly roots ideas in the hearts which could not be taught to people in hundreds of years of peaceful education."*[75] The Jihadists feel they can teach and propagate the movement quicker with violence than through peaceful education.

The Management of Savagery reveals the Jihadists' views on educating their soldiers. The author shows concern with Jihadist soldiers who infiltrate enemy organizations – such as oil companies, police forces, governments and armies. His concern is that his soldiers may lose piety when surrounded by the infidels over the long periods of time. He recognizes that it takes time to ascend to a position of power. The author desires, but does not describe, an education system that ensures the infiltrated soldier maintains his faith[76]. The desired end state as the author describes it is a soldier who is impervious to suggestion – in other words, brain washed. Brain washing, as described by Edward Hunter in Brain Washing in Red China, is causing a person to draw desired conclusions on their own accord[77]. For the 20th Century Chinese, this meant a person should conclude, on their own, that communism is the solution for China; for the Jihadists, this means the soldier/infiltrator should conclude, on their own, and that the Jihad is the solution for Islam. It is a much more difficult task – keeping a Jihadist focused when he is surrounded by the infidel – than keeping an isolated Chinese citizen devoutly communist. Perhaps this is why the Management of Savagery suggests infiltrated Jihadists are watched by "agents"[78].

The Media and the Internet

Despite the Jihadist's distain for the West's technology-enabled encroachment, use of this technology in the Jihad is indispensable. In the Management of Savagery, the author states

---

[75] Management of Savagery. 55-57
[76] Ibid 52
[77] Hunter, 6
[78] Management of Savagery, 52

that the media will be used with the purpose of attracting large numbers of people to *"join the Jihad, offer support and adopt a negative attitude toward those who do not join the ranks"* and *"push enemy soldiers to join the ranks of the mujahids or at least flee from service of the enemy."*[79] The Jihadists rely on the media to communicate with the masses – not just for recruitment and support but also for justification for their operations. The Management of Savagery explains that the media plan must show justification, in accordance with the Shariah, to the masses for their actions. The author continues to point out that the masses are their support for the future[80]. Understanding what themes the Jihadists use to propagate their ideology is important to developing countermeasures to confront it. To better understand these themes and gain an appreciation for how the Jihadists use the global media, I attended an expert's panel entitled "Inside the Mind of a Terrorist"[81].

One of the panelists was Doctor Mohammed M. Hafez. He is a Professor in the Department of Political Science at the University of Missouri – Kansas City. He authored the books *Why Muslims Rebel: Repression and Resistance in the Islamic World* (2003) and *Manufacturing Human Bombs: The Making of Palestinian Suicide Bombers* (2006). Hafez teaches courses on *Islam and World Politics*, *Politics of the Middle East*, and *Terrorism and Political Violence*. Hafez explains how the Jihadists market their ideology through propaganda and terrorism. The Jihadists, he says, deliberately target political activists for their cause. They pay close attention to demographics – they seek modern, successful and educated Muslim activists for all operations – especially suicide bombings. The more an individual has to live for the more powerful a statement his intentionally death makes. The death of the suicide bomber actually inspires others to follow suit. This is in keeping with The Management of Savagery's educations strategies of *"Education through Pious Deed, Example or Momentous Event"* The

---

[79] Management of Savagery, 22 (of the original document)
[80] Ibid.
[81] Panel Discussion *"Inside the Mind of a Terrorist"* conducted at Fort Leavenworth on 26 October, 2006.

recruitment of suicide bombers is important to the Jihad because it inspires so many. Recruiting

suicide bombers receives special attention and generally follows five primary themes: *Devotion to*

faith, the bomber is extraordinary in his dedication to faith; *Sacrifice,* the bomber has personal

wealth and family; has much to live for on earth but sacrifices it all for God and is rewarded with

eternal life in paradise; *Eagerness,* the bomber cannot wait to be called to kill himself in the jihad;

Success, regardless of the outcome in his attack, disinformation provides an exaggerated amount

of damage. It is not uncommon for subsequent propaganda messages to claim 200 American

deaths in a single attack; *Dream Visions,* the bomber is spoken to by God in his dreams and God

has promised paradise.

Hafez explained that Jihadist recruiting propaganda strategy is designed to follow this

sequential logic: Gain attention to the problem through *Agitation Propaganda* or *Hate*

Propaganda; Identify the source of the problem through *Disinformation* or *Black Propaganda*;

Propose the solution (i.e. the cause) and recruit with *Integration Propaganda.*[82]

Hafez showed a variety of themes common in Jihadist propaganda. The variety of

themes attracts different Muslims, depending on the recipient's background or status. Nearly all

the themes address emotional appeals. *Agitation* and *Hate Propaganda* uses humiliation of

Muslims for powerful emotional appeal. The Islamic civilization has a long, proud history so

humiliation and shame stir up powerful emotions. When the brotherhood of Muslims is

humiliated or shamed it calls for the entire society to feel humiliated and shamed. Typical images

of *Agitation* and *Hate Propaganda* show dead Muslim women and children or Muslims living in

extreme poverty. Other popular themes include Americans' desecration of the Quran, disrespect

for holy sites or the humiliation of Muslims during the Abu Graib prison scandal (see Appendix

Four). *Disinformation* and *Black Propaganda* are used to identify the cause of the shame and

humiliation. Typical propaganda messages depict America, Israel and "illegitimate" Muslim

---

[82] I have combined Cunningham's propaganda categories with Dr. Hafez's observations of Jihadist propaganda strategy.

leaders as the cause of the problems. Propaganda images show infidel leaders shaking hands, kissing, or celebrating with apostate Muslim leaders while doing nothing to help the poor, suffering and down trodden Muslims. Apostate leaders are shown to be disinterested or indifferent to the shame and humiliation depicted with exaggerated or untrue accounts of Americans mishandling or searching Muslim women. *Integration Propaganda* calls Muslims to the Jihad. This propaganda theme calls for the vigilante-style justice that none but the Jihadists will provide. Images and themes depict Jihadist heroes and martyrs fighting on behalf of the weak and helpless.[83] This propaganda slightly alters the neorevivalists propaganda, which always accentuated the social problems of the West like prostitution, alcoholism, crime and sexual promiscuity.[84].

The Internet has provided the Jihadists with a way to communicate with Muslims worldwide. The images, videos and music of the Jihad are developed, disseminated and received globally. Understanding the messages of the Jihad requires cultural deciphering. Providing that expertise at the *"Inside the Mind of a Terrorist"* panel was Mr. Afshon Ostovar. Ostovar serves as an associate at the Combating Terrorism Center at the United States Military Academy at West Point. His research interests include political Islamic movements, propaganda, and the intellectual and cultural history of the Middle East. He has published *Visual Motifs in Jihadi Internet Propaganda* through the Combating Terrorism Center at West Point, and is currently designing curricula on Islamist terrorism for the FBI. Ostovar's contribution to the panel was his explanation of the meanings of Jihadist art. Images draw upon cultural knowledge and communicate emotions like the faces of martyrs in heaven, pride in found associated with images of lions, the eternal paradise depicted in nature (see Appendix Four). Visual propaganda disseminated via the internet communicate much in the same way Mao Tse-Tung's propaganda

---

[83] Inside the Mind of a Terrorist panel
[84] Esposito, 154-155

posters and art communicated with the Chinese during the Chinese Revolution. Like Mao, the

Jihadists use art to communicate political themes or recruitment propaganda[85].

Summary

Ideology of the Global Jihad has evolved over the past century. It was devised as a

solution to the backwardness of Islamic societies – a solution that called for Muslims to return to

the Shariah and return to preeminence through piety. The West, in particular America, was seen

as a threat to the culture because its materialistic ways distract from traditional Muslim values.

Jihad was expressed as a way to free Muslims from oppression and give them the freedom to

follow the Shariah. The ideology was utopian. Following the Cold War, it was altered into a

vigilante movement reliant on terrorism. Osama Bin Laden and his followers manipulated the

Neorevivalist ideology into a doctrine that only destroys America and the West; it neglects to

solve the social problems of the Islamic Nation. Destruction of America does not cause a

universal implementation of the Shariah. Regardless, the movement continues and is completely

reliant on popularity. Popularity is maintained through propaganda. The most prevalent form of

propaganda is *Deed Propaganda* carried out by the Islamic militants or military forces. Deeds

and examples of sacrifice propagate the ideology through revenge taken against a hated enemy –

the United States. The Jihadists like Mao, recognize education as a necessary means of

propagating the ideology.

The Jihad is not the means to an end – it is the desired end in itself. The Jihadists rely on

the West's free media and internet to recruit support for the Jihad. They follow logic of

Humiliation caused by America, Israel with the assistance of apostate Muslim leaders, *Integrates*

and *Unites Muslims* for a global Jihad as the only possible *Solution.*

---

[85] Inside the Mind of a Terrorist panel

WEAKNESSES TO EXPLOIT

We have examined two social revolutions, Mao's China and the Global Jihadist's. Forty years following the conclusion of the Chinese Revolution, we can see why it was successful: good ideology, sensible strategy, political army, enhanced (but focused) education, and enhanced (but controlled) media. What will we say about the Jihadist revolution forty years from now? It is completely possible that such discussions will never occur, not in an age where terrorists can strike America, possibility with weapons of mass destruction. The Global Jihad will probably die a natural death – the concern is that it will take some of the West with it. The Jihad is reliant on propaganda to maintain is vital popularity. We seek to separate the Jihadists from their support base much in the same way a counter-insurgent force seeks to separate the insurgent from the population[86]. This however, must be done on a global scale. By combating their propaganda, we can significantly curb the movement. To do so we need to develop information strategy that exploits the Jihadist weaknesses – this can be done and it is not as difficult as China.

Weaknesses in Ideology

The current Jihadist ideology, as manipulated by Osama Bin Laden, is not an egalitarian philosophy – it is more centered on the destruction of the United States than it is to providing for the people of Islam. Mao's ideology was genuinely designed to alleviate the Chinese people from their backwards, feudal existence. Mao sought to accomplish this by modernizing China and competing with the West in industry. If successful, China would undergo real development and deliver the nation to the 20th Century. If today's China were any indicator, one would agree that the modernization (not without difficulties like the Great Leap Forward and the Cultural Revolution) was successful. By contrast, Bin Laden's ideology is not egalitarian nor is it all inclusive of the population. His version fails to deliver Muslims from their suffering; his ideology

---

[86] FM 3-24, <u>Counterinsurgency</u> (Headquarters, Department of the Army: December 2006) downloaded 15 March, 2007 from site: http://www.leavenworth.army.mil/ p 1-23

calls for the destruction of the United States. Even if that were possible, that in and of itself would not install the caliphate and Islamic law. Also consider that Islam is a wide spread religion with much diversity across the globe. Interpretation of Islam varies greatly from Africa to the Middle East to Asia. Bin Laden represents a very small faction of militant Islamists; it is unlikely that these people will ever govern with the permission of the people. Osama Bin Laden cannot deliver the kind of leadership Mao delivered in China. Understanding Islam and reading the analyzing the neorevivalist thoughts explain this constraint.

In his writings, Qutb discusses the sovereignty of God in great detail. There can be no worship of man – only God. Because no man can rule over another, (hence the illegitimacy of man's law) there can be no exalted leader of the religion or the ideology. There have not been any powerful religious leaders since the age of the Caliphate. Powerful Islamic leadership has been in short supply since the 13th Century when Genghis Khan overran Baghdad, slaughtered its inhabitants and executed the caliph and his family[87]. This is in stark contrast with the West where, over the ages, powerful charismatic leaders adopted ideologies and led their nations in times of war – sometimes with disastrous results. Without an Islamic version of Lenin, Hitler, Stalin, or Mao, the Islamists have a difficult time unifying their people under the direction and leadership of any one charismatic person. That is not to say that the Islamic people do not share common concerns – they do. Generally, Muslims are disturbed by the actions (and to some the mere existence) of the State of Israel. All agree there is an injustice but none agrees on what to do or who to follow in rectifying the problems. They are unified in emotion but not in action. Islamic Jihadists do not rely solely on a person or state to propagate their ideology; they must rely on the commonality of emotion. Right now, that commonality is hate for the United States. Hate is not enough.

---

[87] Esposito, 60.

Co-opting parts of the Jihadist ideology may offer a chance to separate some of the loyal supporters of the Jihad. In <u>Islam: The Straight Path</u>, Esposito describes the teachings of Muhammad Iqbal. Iqbal, a lawyer in the early 20th Century, rediscovered the principles and values that could be employed in a modern Islamic society. The beliefs of brotherhood and equality of all Muslims was a principle known in Western democracies. He discovered Islamic versions of democracy and parliamentary government. He concluded that democracy was in fact an Islamic idea and the institutions could easily be adapted to Islamic government.[88] This is a perfect theme to use when countering Jihadist propaganda. Not only does this message contribute to modernization of the Islamic world but also provides religious support for this Western idea. Most importantly, it has the potential *create* ideology thus completing the destruction of the Jihadists' ideology. "Islamic Democracy" fills the void Jihadist ideology is damaged or destroyed in the war of ideas.

The logic of the Jihadist ideology is that the destruction of America will isolate Islam from the rest of the Jahiliyyah societies. What the Jihadists overlook is the amazingly successful history of the Islamic civilization when in communication with rest of the world. Islam has had a huge influence in the world by trading, communicating, and sharing with the West and other cultures. Esposito rightly points out that the Jihadists do not realize how human reasoning and sociohistorical exchange has influenced the Islamic civilization. Conversely, the civilizations of Africa, Europe and Asia have benefited from exchange with Muslims. Do they forget how African Sufism came to be or how the Mongol conquerors actually embraced Islam? [89] History shows that contact with Islam has had more influence on more people than war or terrorism. Isolation in order to live under Islamic law does not advance the civilization as easily as opening the society and sharing the religion and culture.

---

[88] Esposito, 140
[89] Ibid 155-156, 126

Weaknesses in Strategy of Propagation

The current Jihadist propaganda strategy is reliant on: hatred for America and her allies, acts of violence against America and her allies, vast media exposure of those violent acts. The exposure then generates interest and admiration in the cause which, in turn, results in money and recruits for the Global Jihad. This strategy is self-perpetuating but creates nothing but violence. Mao's strategy created institutions that governed the people of China. Mao's strategy created schools, improved literacy – all in an effort that encouraged modernization through communism. Modernization and industrialization in China was not a byproduct, it was the purpose. The Jihadist strategy of today only creates destruction and, following the attacks on 9/11, has engaged the Islamic people in war. This strategy has altered the Neorevivalist philosophy.

Seyyid Qutb called for Muslims to fight tyranny to allow a Muslim the freedom of choice to follow the straight path and live in accordance with the Shariah. Although Qutb wrote, "fight" he clearly intended for the battle and jihad to be conducted against oppression and non-violently when possible. By most accounts, democracy and rule of law is the opposite of tyranny. Tyrants do poorly in free, multi-party elections. Qutb's strategy called for a demonstration of piety and strength in faith to deliver people to the straight path. Qutb's was a strategy of leading by example, not by force. Osama Bin Laden has been accused of "hijacking" Islam – it can also be said the he also hijacked the neorevivalist ideology. Violence is a weakness in strategy.

Weaknesses with the Military

One significant weakness of the Jihadist military's method of propagation is that it lacks the structural backing of a legitimate government. Mao Tse-Tung's military philosophy was that the Red Army and politics were inseparable. Mao combined the government and the military to deliver an effective "one-two" punch when propagating the ideology of the communists. The Red Army could control a Chinese village and introduce the ideology by force if necessary. The Chinese government would eventually assume the role of retaining that village with law, rules and supervision. The Jihadists lack the governmental component. The Jihadist military and Jihadist policy are closely woven but the lack of governance leaves the ideology without the ability to retain. Strict enforcement of the Shariah is temporary as there is a lacking of vital governmental institutions to maintain the society. The Jihadists therefore must perpetually conduct acts of terrorism to propagate their ideology.

Terrorist action by the Jihad's military is required to propagate the ideology. It is a difficult entity to combat as terrorists can operate in a society like a parasite. To fight war, they do not need to manufacture weapons, munitions or delivery systems – they will use what is already created. They do not to manufacture communications, media, cameras, or computers – they will utilize ours against us. They do not need to succeed every time – they only need to succeed once. The military creates information that is reported by the infrastructure that communicates the ideology to the support base that provides money and recruits to the jihad – all the Jihadists need to do is conduct violence. The globalized world will do the rest for them. Fortunately, for the West, not all of the Jihadists' acts of terror are popular. The killing of fellow Muslims, suicide bombings and beheadings are examples of unpopular acts of terror that can condemn the movement. These mistakes should be highlighted in our information operations and be made to represent the entire movement. The military system of the Global Jihad is its strongest entity. Killing every terrorist is impossible; cutting him off from his support base is the only plausible solution[90]. The weakness to exploit is to interrupt the propaganda flow and stop the cycle.

In Management of Savagery, it was noted by the author that Jihadist infiltrators operating within the apostate government might be susceptible to "losing piety" while operating amongst the infidels. To prevent the conversion to infidel, the author alluded to brainwashing the infiltrators to insure they will perform their Jihadist duties when called. Hunter examined how the Chinese brainwashed its citizens and workers in his book Brainwashing in Red China. On page

---

[90] FM3-24, 1-23.

15 of his work, Hunter describes how the Chinese would force its citizens to keep diaries. In the diary, a person was to produce intimate thoughts about communism, and self reflect on his or her own weaknesses in being communist. The diaries were inspected by party workers. On the surface, it appeared like an inaccurate and hokey way to for the government to read a person's mind, after all, the person could simply lie in his diary. Under the surface was a more complex purpose. The repetition of thought and writing would eventually change the person's mind. Through repetition, a person will eventually go from phony to sincere[91]. This method of reflection could easily be administered to members of the government, military, police and industry workers in the battleground states such as Iraq and Afghanistan. The intention is to strengthen the resolve of the legitimate workers and reduce the numbers of Jihadist infiltrators.

Weaknesses with Education and Literacy

According to Cunningham, education is the natural enemy of propaganda. Education can only occur when a person has had the opportunity to investigate all sides of an issue and make a free decision or assessment.[92] It is fair to assume Cunningham would not concur with the conclusion that Mao educated his people; Mao only offered the communist version of information, i.e. propaganda. Mao's ability to convert the people of China through education is largely absent in the Jihadist movement. Mao educated the masses so that they could read and understand communism – this was done in a closed environment, one that was effectively sealed off from the rest of the world. China recognized the importance of studying science and technology so that China would someday compete with the West in the modern, industrialized world. The Jihadists use education to create devout fighters who must find all knowledge in Islam. Jihadists can only accomplish this educational feat in small, ungoverned regions or failed states whereas China's totalitarian regime could isolate their entire country from the ideas and

---

[91] Hunter, 15 – 17.
[92] Cunningham, 184-185.

thoughts emanating from the West. For the Jihadists, education is a two-way street. A child educated and indoctrinated in a Madrasah may embody the Jihadist cause, or, his literacy may cause him to think for himself when exposed to the free and open world society that results from globalization. The closed, isolated nature of 20th Century China is difficult to replicate today.

Based on attacks like the bombing of the Baghdad Book Market, and the doctrine expressed in <u>Management of Savagery</u>, it appears the Jihadists need their people to be illiterate and ignorant to Western education. Mao had the resources to isolate China from the West but the Jihadists do not. Advancements in global communications, internet and satellite television make isolation nearly impossible – especially since most Muslim nations already have the infrastructure in place. Our information operations should exploit this vulnerability by insuring all "Western" information is easily accessible to Middle Eastern computers. Western news, Universities, and databases should be available in Arabic and easily located by Arabic search engines. Computers with links to the modern world should be more and more accessible. Inexpensive computers with wireless connectivity throughout the Middle East will allow Muslims access to an alternative message – that of progress through education and modernization.

Weaknesses with the Media

Mao Tse-Tung realized that news, art and entertainment were important to the Chinese Revolution. The Jihadists too realize that people are influenced by what they see and hear on television, print, radio and computer. Today it appears that the Jihadists are making more effort to influence via the media than that of the United States or Western governments. Art, as depicted in Annex 4, shows the powerful emotions that inspire Muslims to join the Jihad. How difficult would it be for the United States government to contract modern Muslim artists to create similar works that propagate the ideology of modernization? It is obvious that American money, technology, computer graphics, and marketing knowledge combined with modern Islamic artists could produce compelling works for the internet, television and print. The airwaves in most of the

Middle East are free – the West needs only to occupy that space with effective messages that are informative, interesting and entertaining. Moderate Muslims run a terrible risk at producing modern or Western style programming but it is slowly developing.

Discovery Times, a cable channel available in the United States, recently ran a documentary entitled "TV Iraqi Style". The one-hour program described how Iraqis are receiving interesting, modern television shows for the first time. During the Saddam era, television programming was strictly censored and dedicated to the idolization of Saddam Hussein. Since the fall of the regime, the Iraqi television industry has taken off. One popular television show is "Iraqi Idol" which, like its American counterpart, is largely a talent show. Most of the performers sing traditional Iraqi music.[93] This illustrates that Iraqis can modernize while maintaining traditions. Conversely, insurgents frequently target Iraqi actors or television personalities to terrorize the industry with the purpose of restricting free speech and dissuading the industry from propagating modernization. Regardless, Iraqi entertainers continue to produce programming and ratings continue to climb. Commercials or public service announcements calling for peace, compromise and modernization would reach a huge number of viewers – especially during curfews when the ratings are at their highest[94].

Satellite television has made a great breakthrough since the fall of Saddam Hussein. Satellite television requires very little investment on behalf of the producer and little technical training on behalf of the operators. With a little cash and knowledge, anyone can broadcast a television program and reach millions. One such television station broadcasts from inside Iraq. Al-Zawraa is a satellite TV station that is somewhat indicative of MTV in that it plays video after video of insurgent attacks on American forces. It is a propaganda network that constantly broadcasts slogans and visual icons followed by graphic videos. The Iraqi government has been powerless to stop it. The broadcasters are too illusive. Cheap new technologies allow the

---

[93] "TV Iraqi Style", Discovery Times, aired 13 November 2006.
[94] Ibid.

insurgent propaganda broadcasters allow the producers to hide effectively and avoid capture[95].

This form of propaganda is powerful – it is emotionally inspired. Graphic attacks are viewed as revenge against the United States, alleviating much of the ingrained hatred. The attacks spawn support and continue the cycle of violence in the Jihad. If satellite television is simple and economical to produce, is it fair to assume the United States government could contract modern Iraqis to produce competing programs. As with education and webpage design, American technology experience and expertise should be able to develop far superior programming (like an Iraqi version of "Cops"?) that supports the Iraqi government and a movement to modernize Iraq.

Summary

There are significant weaknesses in the Jihadist ideology. Osama Bin Laden has "hijacked" the neorevivalist ideology by omitting the original egalitarian (albeit utopian) motivation. Their strategy is reliant on violence; it may serve in the short term as emotional gratification but it fails to return Islam to preeminence. The Jihadist ideology fails to address future governance or modernization of the Islamic people, it only focuses on the destruction of the United States. That alone cannot advance the Islamic people. The fact that there is not an undisputed unified leader of the Jihad should be exploited. Alternative ideologies such as the idea of "Islamic Democracy" exist and should be co-opted into a new ideology that receives the support from legitimate governments worldwide. The Jihadist military is its strongest entity but it lacks a legitimate government to retain political gains of military action. The Jihadists lack the governmental institutions the guarantee a continuance of change. Education, now that it has started, is difficult to stop or contain. Globalized communications allow Muslims unprecedented access to legitimate information as well as propaganda. Our task is to enable those Muslims to access information easily through language barriers and infrastructure. The use of television

---

[95] Liz Sly, "Graphic U.S. Deaths Broadcast in Iraq", <u>Chicago Tribune</u>, 25 February 2007 accessed 26 February 2007 from site: <u>https://www.us.army.mil/suite/earlybird/Feb2007/e20070226492419.html</u>

programming, traditional and satellite open a "free speech" zone where the Jihadists have taken the initiative. With American help, modern Islamic television can broadcast high quality programming that promotes peaceful modernization.

CONCLUSION

The Jihadists are reliant on propaganda because they do not have the kind of control over society that was necessary for China's revolution. Propaganda communicates an ideology that is based on hatred and the popularity of the movement. Popularity and public opinion are fickle things and can be manipulated. The disapproving worldwide opinion of the United States may take time to repair but that does not mean the Jihadist propaganda message should be left alone until then. The

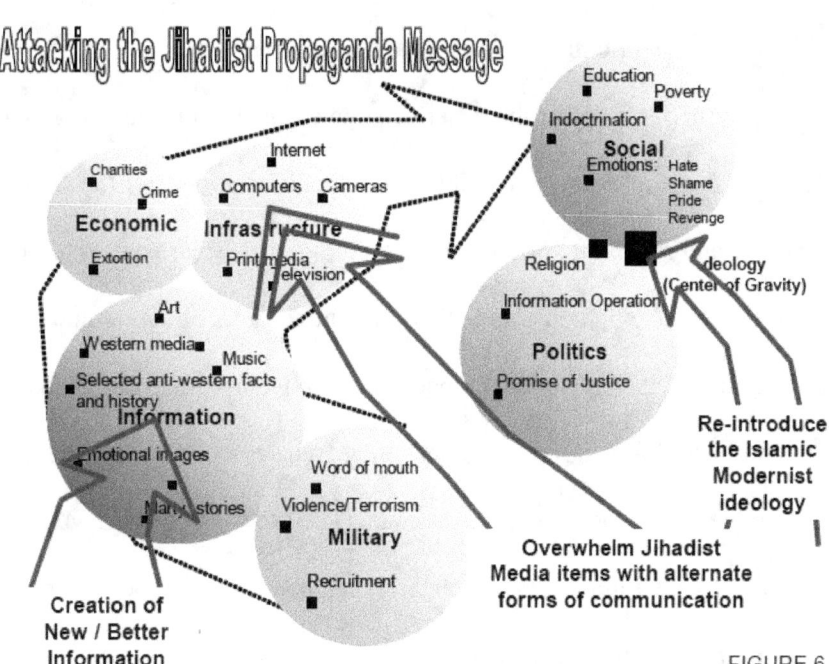

FIGURE 6

Jihadist message should be attacked along three avenues of approach: the information system, the infrastructure and the ideology. Figure 6 show that the Jihadists maintain their movement with military (terrorist) action. They "create" propaganda or, information (*Education by Momentous Event* and *Education by Example*[96]) of a popular nature which is picked up by the infrastructure (global media, internet, satellite TV etc) and is transmitted to the social system. The social system provides people, funding and support to the political system that, in turn, supports the military

---

[96] See chapter three

51

and the cycle continues. To stop or mitigate the propaganda flow is to critically injure the entire movement.

Injuring the movement is not enough. To destroy the dangerous Jihadist ideology means it needs to be replaced. Destruction is only completed with creation of something else. The Islamic civilization needs to return to a reputable stature in the world before this war will truly be over. Resurgence in Islamic modernization, as initiated in the early 20th Century during the colonial period, needs to become the ideology for Muslim societies. Advancements in science, technology and governance will not only benefit their society but will also improve all the societies of the world in this new globalized environment.

America, not just the American Government, must take action in the information war fought on the very airwaves and internet it created. Support for the Global Jihadists, in the terms of money and recruiting, occurs on the same internet America uses to bolster its cyber economy. Video, music, photography, and other influential forms of communication bolster the Jihadist's ideology and calls for Muslims support the war against America. By comparison, in America, the same influential forms of communication are used to compel customers to part with their money. The people of America, Madison Avenue, Hollywood, YouTube, MySpace, media and the multitude of other information producers, can make a difference in this ideological war. Instead, these information producers and communicators focus on scandals, gossip, and mindless entertainment. We are ignorant of the Jihadist ideology and methods. We are excessively naïve and inadvertently but continuously play into the Jihadist strategy. According to Malcolm Gladwell, a great idea can spread like an epidemic. In his book Tipping Point, Gladwell explores social epidemics and concludes that an idea and the right amount of resources accurately focused on key areas will initiate an epidemic[97]. Which epidemic do we want?

---

[97] Malcolm Gladwell, The Tipping Point, (New York: Little, Brown and Company 2000) 255.

APPENDIX 1 World War I

WWI propaganda emphasized Christianity and democracy to stir the emotions of the public. This emphasis called on men to act in the greater good. Interestingly, both sides were Christian and both had democratic backgrounds.

America
Category: Agitation
Technique: Appeal to Emotion
Goal: Fundraising

England
Category: Integration
Technique: Appeal to Emotion
Goal: Recruitment

Germany
Category: White
Technique: Appeal to Emotion
Goal: Recruitment

America
Category: Disinformation
Technique: Style, reason
Goal: Resources

England
Category: Hate
Technique: Style
Goal: Recruitment

Source:

APPENDIX 2 World War II

WWII propaganda emphasized race and fear over the ideals of Christianity and democracy. Hate and fear inspired recruitment as well as industrial production. WWII propaganda still shapes how today's generation thinks of the "last good war" or the "greatest generation".

America
Category: Integration
Technique: Appeal to Emotion, style
Goal: Recruitment

USSR
Category: Integration
Technique: Appeal to Emotion, style
Goal: Recruitment

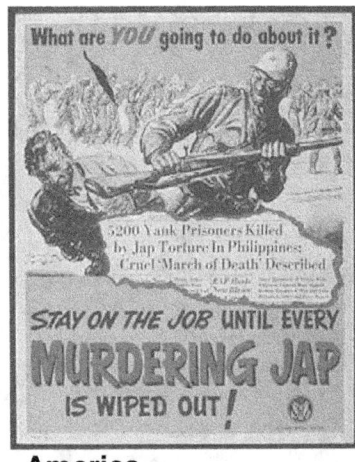

America
Category: Hate
Technique: Appeal to Emotion, style
Goal: Production

Germany
Category: Hate, Agitation
Technique: Appeal to Emotion, Diversion
Goal: Ideology

America
Category: Hate, Integration
Technique: Appeal to Emotion, style
Goal: Production

APPENDIX 3 Communist China

China's propaganda evolved during the period of social revolution. In the beginning it called on people to support the military actions of the communists. Later, it focused on modernization and economy. Mao's used propaganda to convince his people that life under communism was good and China was advancing by leaps and bounds.

China 1949
Category: Integration, White
Technique: Appeal to Emotion, style
Goal: Unity, "Cult of Personality"

China 1959
Category: White or Bureaucratic
Technique: Appeal to Emotion, style
Goal: Production, Unity

把更多的鋼鐵
送到祖國建設的最前線

China 1955?
Category: Bureaucratic, White
Technique: Falsehood, Emotion
Goal: Change society from agrarian to industrial

China 1960?
Category: Bureaucratic, White
Technique: Falsehood, Emotion
Goal: Faith in Collective Farming program

APPENDIX 4 Jihadist Propaganda

Jihadist propaganda relies on hate to agitate the Islamic population. Powerful emotions like shame are common themes. The Jihadists call on Muslims to exact revenge on America through their version of Jihad. Jihadists use suicide bombers to educate the public with "pious deed" or "example". Inspiration from this sacrifice draws new recruits globally.

Jihadist
Category: Hate, Agitation
Technique: Appeal to Emotion- Shame, Revenge
Goal: Anger population, unify against America

Jihadist
Category: Hate, Agitation
Technique: Appeal to Emotion- Fear
Goal: Anger population, unify against America and Israel

Jihadist
Category: Integration
Technique: Appeal to Emotion- Pride
Goal: Join the Jihad, Fight America

Jihadist
Category: Integration
Technique: Appeal to Emotion- Pride
Goal: Join the Jihad, fight for Iraq and Islam

Jihadist
Category: Integration
Technique: Appeal to Emotion- Pride, respect
Goal: Martyrdom – become a suicide bomber for the Jihad or Sacrifice for the good of Islam

Source: Terrorist Expert Panel Mr. Afshon Ostovar 26 October, 2006

BIBLIOGRAPHY

Aboul-Enein, Youssef *Sheikh Abdel-Fatah Al-Khalidi Revitalizes Sayid Qutb*, accessed 1 March, 2007 from site: http://www.ctc.usma.edu/Khalidi-Qutb3.pdf.

Al Qaeda's Fatwa, Online News Hour, accessed 1 March 2007 from site: http://www.pbs.org/newshour/terrorism/international/fatwa_1998.html.

Analysis Madrassas, PBS Front Line, accessed 7 March 2007 from site: http://www.pbs.org/wgbh/pages/frontline/shows/saudi/analyses/madrassas.html.

Arendt, Hannah, The Origins of Totalitarianism, (New York: Hartcourt Brace & Company, 1979).

Aaron, Jane E. The Little, Brown Compact Handbook, 3rd Edition (New York: Longman 1998).

Bin Laden's Fatwa, Online News Hour, accessed 1 March 2007 from site: http://www.pbs.org/newshour/terrorism/international/fatwa_1996.html.

Chinese propaganda posters and commentary downloaded 15 February 2007 from site: http://www.iisg.nl/exhibitions/chairman/chn01.php.

Clausewitz, Carl. On War, Howard, Michael, and Paret, Peter, Eds., Trans., (New York: Everyman's, 1993).

Commander's Handbook for an Effects-Based Approach to Joint Operations, (Joint Warfighting Center, Suffolk Virginia 2006).

Conserva, Henry, Propaganda Techniques, (Bloomington Illinois: 1st Books Library,2003).

Cunningham, Stanley B. The Idea of Propaganda: A Reconstruction. , (Westport Connecticut: Praeger Publishers, 2002).

Dictionary.com. *The American Heritage® Dictionary of the English Language, Fourth Edition*, Houghton Mifflin Company, 2004. http://dictionary.reference.com/browse/propaganda (accessed: December 01, 2006).

Esposito, John L. Islam: The Straight Path, Third Edition, (New York, Oxford: Oxford University Press, 2005).

FM 3-24, Counterinsurgency (Headquarters, Department of the Army: December 2006) downloaded 15 March, 2007 from site: http://www.leavenworth.army.mil/.

Fromkin, David, Peace to End All Peace, (New York: Henry Holt and Company, 1989).

Gladwell, Malcolm The Tipping Point, (New York: Little, Brown and Company 2000).

Houn, Franklin, To Change a Nation: Propaganda and Indoctrination in Communist China, (New York: Crowell-Collier Publishing, 1961).

Hunter, Edward Brain Washing in Red China, the Calculated Destruction of Men's Minds, (New York: The Vanguard Press, 1951).

Huntington, Samuel P. The Clash of Civilizations and Remaking of World Order, (New York: Simon and Schuster, 1996).

Interview with Colonel Hu, Chinese Liaison Officer, Combined Arms Center, Fort Leavenworth Kansas (5 December, 2006).

Interview with Dr Will McCants conducted in conjunction with a panel discussion on Inside the Mind of a Terrorist. Panel and interview conducted 26 October, 2006.

Joint Publication 3-0 Joint Operations accessed 25 February 2007 from site: www.dtic.mil/doctrine.

Joint Pub 3-53, Doctrine for Joint Psychological Operations 10 July 1996.

Lind, William S. and Nightengale, Keith Colonel *The Changing Face of War: Into the Fourth Generation*, Marine Corps Gazette, 1989.

Management of Savagery, The, translated by Dr Will McCants, (Harvard University:John M. Olin Institute for Strategic Studies, 23 May, 2006).

Middle East Section, New York Times accessed 6 March, 2007 from site: http://www.nytimes.com/2007/03/06/world/middleeast/06cnd-troops.html?_r=1&hp&oref=slogin.

Qutb, Seyyid Milestones, (Damascus, Syria: Dar Al-Ilm, 1960?).

Reference Writers: Anna Louise Strong, accessed 15 December, 2007 from site: http://www.marxists.org/glossary/people/s/t.htm#strong-anna-louise.

Sly, Liz "Graphic U.S. Deaths Broadcast in Iraq", Chicago Tribune, 25 February 2007 accessed 26 February 2007 from site: https://www.us.army.mil/suite/earlybird/Feb2007/e20070226492419.html.

Sulzberger, C. L., The American Heritage Picture History of World War II, (New York: Random House, 1994).

Terrorist Tactics, Operation Iraqi Freedom accessed 3 March 2007 from site: http://www.mnf-iraq.com/index.php?option=com_content&task=view&id=727&Itemid=44.

Tse-Tung, Mao, The Selected Works of Mao Tse-Tung, Volume One 1926-1936, (New York: International Publishers, 1954).

Tse-Tung, Mao, The Selected Works of Mao Tse-Tung, Volume Three 1939-1941, (New York: International Publishers, 1954).

Tse-Tung, Mao Selected Works of Mao Tse-Tung, Volume Five 1945 – 1949, (New York: International Publishers, 1954).

"TV Iraqi Style", Discovery Times, aired 13 November 2006.

Wikipedia.com, *Truth*, available at: http://en.wikipedia.org/wiki/Truth (accessed: December 4, 2006).

Winger, J. and Baggett, B., The Great War and the Shaping of the 20th Century, (New York: Penguin Studio, 1996).

World War I propaganda posters downloaded 10 January 2007 from site: http://www.firstworldwar.com/posters/index.htm.